Giovanni Arena

La città 6 dell'E42

Giovanni Arena

La città 6 dell'E42

Grandi esposizioni nel ventennio

Edizioni Sant'Antonio

Imprint
Any brand names and product names mentioned in this book are subject to trademark, brand or patent protection and are trademarks or registered trademarks of their respective holders. The use of brand names, product names, common names, trade names, product descriptions etc. even without a particular marking in this work is in no way to be construed to mean that such names may be regarded as unrestricted in respect of trademark and brand protection legislation and could thus be used by anyone.

Cover image: Fornito dall'autore

Publisher:
Edizioni Accademiche Italiane
is a trademark of
International Book Market Service Ltd., member of OmniScriptum Publishing Group
17 Meldrum Street, Beau Bassin 71504, Mauritius

Printed at: see last page
ISBN: 978-620-2-00055-0

Giovanni Arena

La città 6 dell'E42

Grandi esposizioni nel ventennio

Indice

Introduzione
The city number 6 of the World Fair of Rome E42 4

Esporre il primato italiano 37

Icone di Roma antica 47

Destino imperiale 57

Documenti, monumenti 60

Appendice 65

Bibliografia essenziale (fonti primarie - fonti secondarie) 90

Elenco delle Fonti e delle Abbreviazioni

ABEL	Archivio Bruno Ernesto Lapadula, Roma
ACS	Archivio Centrale di Stato, Roma
AMAE	Archivio Storico-Diplomatico del Ministero degli Affari Esteri, Roma
AMDO	Archivio storico-architettonico Mostra d'Oltremare, Napoli
APM	Archivio Plinio Marconi, Roma
ASMAI	Archivio Storico del Ministero dell'Africa Italiana
ASNA	Archivio di Stato, Napoli
Dc	Documentario
GL	Giornale luce
GP	Gabinetto Prefettura
ICRS	Istituto Campano per la Storia della Resistenza "Vera Lombardi", Napoli
LUCE	Archivio Storico dell'Istituto Luce, Roma
MCP	Ministero della Cultura Popolare
MSP	Ministero stampa e propaganda
PCM	Presidenza del Consiglio dei Ministri
SPDco	Segreteria particolare del duce, carteggio ordinario
WG	Archivio Wolfsoniana - Fondazione regionale per la Cultura e lo Spettacolo, Gen

All. =
alleg
ato;
b. =
bust
a; f.
=
fasci
o; fasc. = fascicolo;
rapp. = rappresentazione

Introduction

The city number 6 of the World Fair of Rome E42

The story of the Triennale d'Oltremare (1938-1940), the last Italian colonial exhibition, is closely linked to the political and the cultural politics of fascism. The event was conceived as a great colonial exhibition which was to enhance the economic and cultural function of its host, Naples, within the new colonial empire that was being born at the time. The Triennale d'Oltremare aimed to document the work for the conquest of the empire, to illustrate the characteristics of the various zones of the Italian lands overseas, and present the resources of the Motherland in respect of the valuation of lands overseas.

The show was meant as a response to the great Colonial Exposition in Paris of 1931, in which the Italian Fascist government participated, while it had still not completely resolved the problem of Libyan anti-colonial resistance and when it did not yet rule Ethiopia. The number of visitors and the resonance of the 1938-1940 show were, however, much lower than the organizers hoped for. Just a month after the opening on 9 May 1940, Italy entered the war and the exhibition that was supposed to crown a victorious empire was closed. The celebration of the new empire corresponded with the eve of its collapse. What was supposed to represent the cutting edge of colonial fascist propaganda came to be representative of the gap between the aspirations and the means of the Italian colonial policy and the gap between Italy and other colonial powers. This Triennale also integrates various aspects of the art world of its time: art and propaganda; strategy of acquiring consensus and aesthetics of the colonial policies. The exhibition of Naples has a very specific format, powerfully symbolic, and shows an image that overwhelms the architecture. Created in an moment in which each creative act had to be above all a political act, the show was based on the supremacy of the observer through the visual impact of the setting. This text therefore examines the political motivations of staging a great exhibition project, likely to be repeated every three years, in the time of a looming world crisis and looks at the ways the exhibition was intended as a tool for colonial propaganda. At the same time we will try to analyze some aspects related to the museographic and artistic project.

During the 1920s, the interaction between colonial discourse and colonial propaganda in Italy had a special significance for two reasons. First, colonial propaganda was crucial because the Italian colonial empire was not large and soon proved to be expensive to maintain. Therefore it became necessary to create a strong consensus about the imperial status in Italy. The conquest of Ethiopia in 1936 increased the need to create an image of a legendary victory. Secondly, the Italian national identity was weak compared to many other identities circulating in the peninsula, both pre-existing and co-present: regional identities, ideological and religious identities were often stronger than the national one. For reasons intrinsic and extrinsic, the space for colonial propaganda in Italy was large, especially in the period between the two world wars.

What made such propaganda especially important overseas for both liberal and Fascist Italy was the aura of prestige that the State emanated toward the public, and outward to the ensemble of great powers. Italian fascism introduced several novelties, most importantly in this context the breadth and character of the centralist institutions and media which were enabled through colonial propaganda. Exhibitions and colonial museums played an important part in this and they needed to achieve a double aim – to empower the acculturation process overseas and to amplify the support to the colonial policy.

Fascism, which had been on the rise in Italy from the 1920s, strongly accentuated the role of exclusively colonial exhibitions in relation to the construction of a national identity and gave it an unrealistic colonial policy. Prior to that, the important colonial exhibition of Genoa in 1904 was organized to support and promote the cause of expansion events that had been held also in Palermo (1891), Turin (1898), Florence (1903) and Milan (1906). Various events were organised even after the end of the First World War, but it was during the Fascist period that the Ministry of Colonies gave a particular impetus to the organization of colonial exhibitions both in Italy and abroad. Between 1920 and 1940, many book fairs, colonial expositions and exhibitions of colonial art were held for specialists and scholars. Very successful were the First Colonial Art Exhibition in Rome in 1931 and the Second Colonial Art Exhibition in Naples in 1934-35. There were also agricultural fairs and exhibitions of colonial crafts as well as more general colonial exhibitions targeted at non-specialist public that aimed at strengthening the 'colonial consciousness' of the Italians and at reinforcing the myth of Africa. Objects collected by explorers in Africa, 'relics' of soldiers who fell in the field, special ethnographic collections that began to arrive in provincial towns, universities and specialized colonial institutions were organized in the meantime in permanent exhibitions or museums. Simultaneously, African fauna was also brought to zoos around the peninsula.

The structure and content of the early colonial exhibitions that were organized in Italy before 1920 was subjected to general interest in the colonies which took precedence over economic and commercial goals and in essence, propaganda. In contrast, in the colonial exhibitions of the 1930s, a historical-ideological significance moved above the exclusively commercial role of the previous exhibitions. In fact, from simple 'fairs' of the exotic, these events became complex narratives with different levels of communication and reading.

The effectiveness of the new Fascist propaganda in Italy was also put on display in the colonies. An example can be seen in the first Fiera Campionaria di Tripoli (The National Exhibition of Tripoli, 1927), initiated by Benito Mussolini which, therefore, became the first major statement of the economic revival of Tripoli after the military reconquest. The Exhibition aimed at informing the visitors about the colony of Libya – the idea was to create an ephemeral city where small presentations of the local life and labour were constructed alongside many stalls and various regional and community halls. 'Orderly' and 'cleaned-up', the Arabs and Jews of Tripoli were brought within the enclosure of the Exhibition.

The village featured a 'typical' Tripolitan market (*sūq*). The space was full of palm trees and populated by native Libyans who were distributed according to the different activities that they carried out in all the areas of the Fair as attractions for visitors. Silversmiths, goldsmiths, carpet weavers, ivory craftsmen, and manufacturers of thousands of decorative objects worked there in the small space of their shops for two months. Using traditional instruments, they produced silk fabrics, wool and cotton, articles of gold, silver, leather, carpets, Misurata Tauorga mats, household items and ceramics. Next to the *sūq*, there was a reproduction of an Arab house in all its details, an Arabic mill in animal traction and a space used for spinning wool as well as a space for dancers and musicians. Prof. Renato Bartoccini, an expert on Tripolitania classical antiquities, was responsible for the ethnographic exhibition in the Colony - the Arab life was framed here in all its manifestations.

The Fair of Tripoli was repeated in subsequent years and was organized by the *Ente Autonomo Fiera Campionaria di Tripoli* (Autonomous Institute of Tripoli Trade Fair). Starting in 1930, the Fiera Campionaria di Tripoli was officially approved by the Union of International Fairs (UFI), an association founded in Milan in 1925 to bring together the most important national and international organizations in the exhibition sector. With this acknowledgment the Fiera Campionaria di Tripoli was transformed into an international fair and *interafricana,* the first international exhibition in Africa.

The Fair occupied an area of 52,000m^2 and differed in many ways from the earlier trade-oriented exhibitions which, like the Great Exhibition of 1851, used the paradigm of a 'city on show.' Such places participated in the dynamics of the industrial society. Through these colonial exhibitions Fascism gradually appropriated the model used to promote modernist exhibition and its own political ideology. The Fair of Tripoli became a propaganda tool of the privileged regime, which tried to show its colonial conquests and celebrate its colonial history. These early events in Africa continued until the outbreak of World War II and the regime was able to take inspiration from them to achieve similar exposures in Italy. Italian exhibitions were organized using old ideas but with extremely modern forms of communication.

After the 'general rehearsals' of the two events of Tripoli in 1927 and 1928, the first significant colonial exposition organized in Italy was the Mostra Nazionale Coloniale (Colonial National Exhibition) show in Turin in 1928. Many descriptive articles and images published in colonial magazines describe the exhibition, which occupied an extensive area on the left bank of the river Po in the Pilonetto area. There appears to be a large colonnaded portico divided symmetrically by a pavilion from which the streets radiates and connect the exhibition of animal colonies and four colonial villages, each inhabited by natives of the respective colony. Enclosed between the two arms of the arches, the hall of honour dominated the entire complex, the site of which was characterized by marble columns with the fasces. Around the arcade, decorated in tiles, a reconstruction of an African town with a market and craft shops opened to the visitor eyes.

After the Turin exhibition, the dialectic between the colonial discourse and propaganda became exceptionally stronger. In 1930, Belgium celebrated the centenary of its independence with the organization of two exhibitions: the Exposition Coloniale d'Anvers (The Colonial Exposition of Antwerp) and L'Exposition Internationale de Liège (the Industrial Exhibition in Liège). The participation of Italy in both shows, together with 22 other states, can be seen as a part of the large project of intensification of colonial propaganda as well as a move against other colonial powers. The relatively small Italian colonial regime tried to compensate for its size resorting to a greater presence in international colonial exhibition. The exhibition in Antwerp, for instance, which was divided into national pavilions, included activities of valorisation of the colonizing nations which were aimed at enhancing their political, social, economic status and at commercial traffic.

The project of the Italian Pavilion of Antwerp, which, among other things, contained objects from the Colonial Museum of Rome, was designed by architect Giovanni Chevalley. Located near the main entrance to the exhibition, it consisted of a series of buildings with large windows and large skylights. Comparing the aesthetics of the Italian pavilion with the most significant ones of for example the Netherlands, France, Persia and the Belgian Congo, the Italian attempt to impose a reminder of the Roman era was evident. The regime chose to highlight the past and imperial Rome as historical legitimacy of its own colonial ambitions by showing symbols of the ancient empire next to images and objects from the colonies.

One of the most significant aspects of the Italian participation in fairs and exhibitions was to demonstrate its connection to the process of modernization of overseas territories, the development that was viewed as an extension of the economic system of the metropolis. The Italian colonies were represented through displays that illustrated the accomplishments of private and government sponsored companies that were active in the exploitation of natural resources and the organization of local industries. The viability of these industries and the colonial economy in general, however, was questionable. These exhibitions promoted the image of prosperous territories that were systematically undergoing development according to metropolitan standards.

Alongside these exhibits, the results of the substantial financial investment by the Italian government into infrastructures were presented and included the construction of new road networks, the improvement of water supply and health systems and the establishment of public institutions. While neither the political dimension of these exhibitions nor their role as propaganda could have been dismissed, they were more than just visual presentations aimed to encourage further economic development; indeed, they were a marketplace in which the products of Italy's colonial possessions were both put on display and sale.

The second and equally important aspect of the Italian colonial representation in fairs and exhibitions abroad was that they were important vehicles for the representation of indigenous cultures. These cultures were presented in both the content of the exhibits, which included ethnographic studies of the local populations and the display of their indigenous crafts and their means of presentation. From a stylistic point of view, the pavilions were hybrids of vernacular architecture and the architectural conventions of exhibition design, invoking a complex negotiation between indigenous and metropolitan worlds. The identity of the local populations was simultaneously being constructed by the norms of anthropology and ethnography, just as their indigenous craft production was subjected to a substantial redefinition by the Fascist authorities. These exhibitions can thus be understood as an extension of the direct manipulation and control of the native body under the aegis of colonialism.

The complex interaction between the political, economic and

representational discourses in these colonial displays creates a powerful trajectory that builds up towards the *Triennale d'oltremare*.

The *Mostra Triennale delle terre italiane d'Oltremare* (the First Triennial Exhibition of Italian Overseas Territories, 1940) is one of the most spectacular examples of the exhibition of public and private colonial collections in Europe. The Bylaws of the Ente Autonomo 'Triennale d'Oltremare' were approved by the Royal Decree of 4 April 1938, no. 2215 and sent the exhibition plans, officially opened in 1940, to motion. For its establishment the project received financial contributions from many different institutions, such as the General Government of Africa Orientale (east Africa), the governments of Libya and Somalia, the City of Naples, Naples Province, the Provincial Council of Corporations of Naples, and the *Banco di Napoli* (the Bank of Naples).

The *Triennale d'oltremare* and its related imperial politics provide the final, and perhaps most telling example of the evolution that took place in Italian colonial representations in exhibitions and fairs at home and abroad. It was organized to celebrate the expansion of the colonized territory by means of a multifaceted communication approach, abundance of financial resources, modern display techniques and the deployment of well-known propaganda resources concerning the opportunities of Italy's overseas empire.

The Triennale d'Oltremare was presented as the largest and most complete survey of the Italian expansion. Its aim was to contextualize Italy's colonial empire in Africa in relation to the historical legacy of conquest and dominance in the region, linking again the accomplishments of Ancient Rome to the Fascist present. It was also the culmination of a process of the development of colonial exhibitions in Italy and abroad that began around the time of Italy's initial colonial conquest of Eritrea in 1890.

As mentioned above, these representations were part of the Italian government's propagandistic effort to create a greater knowledge of these possessions and assert its image as a major colonial power in the international arena. These activities, often undertaken with the participation of groups of colonial supporters like the *Istituto Coloniale Italiano* (the Italian Colonial Institute), included scientific, statistical and historical expeditions. In particular, the *Istituto Coloniale Italiano* was the promoter of the organization of academic conferences, and the publication of books and periodicals reporting on the Italian colonies. Seen in this context, these exhibitions were a carefully measured political programme that responded to the lack of knowledge and interest of Italian society in its colonial empire in Africa.

The intention of the Italian authorities was also to raise support for their colonial activities by promoting awareness of the realities of the colonization process. This would effectively disarm the idea that Italy's colonies were barren lands with no natural or cultural value. However, these exhibitions were not only intended to create popular support within Italy, they were also aimed at the international public and particularly at other colonizing nations such as Britain and France. In this broader European context, these colonial displays can be understood as a metaphorical compensation for the complex of inferiority, which Italy, as the most recent colonizing nation, carried into the colonial enterprise, and a rhetorical expression of Italy's colonial destiny in Africa.

One of the strongest aspects of the idea behind the Triennale d'Oltremare was its integration with the surrounding topography in the significant historical and cultural landscape of the Fuorigrotta district in Naples. However, in doing so, this urban proposal radically transformed the existing landscape through a systematic programme of transplanting species from Italy's colonial possession. The result of this effort was a hybrid between metropolitan and colonial landscapes.

The fusion of these two contexts, metropolitan and colonial, is evident in the design and layout of the exhibition. These qualities can be seen in the arrangement of the various pavilions, which were linked through a complex structure of streets, fountains and landscape that lent an excellent quality to the site that was evocative of a colonial environment. On the other hand, the generous use of landscape and relaxed spatial planning of the *piano regolatore* (the development plan) of Carlo Cocchia and Luigi Piccinato, the architects who designed the general project of this exhibition, reflected contemporary planning principles, which sought a well-balanced interaction between the building and the environment.

The Fascist regime put a great effort into the organization of the Exhibition. Vincenzo Tecchio was appointed National Director at the head of the teamwork, and the organization was also followed by *Ministero dell'Africa Italiana* (Ministry of Italian Africa). Each sector benefited from the work of counsellors, for instance Carlo Zaghi, Italian journalist and historian, a scholar of colonial Africa and Italy who was responsible for the historical sector. Pietro Badoglio, Italian military general and politician responsible of the war of conquest in Ethiopia who organized the military sector, while Giovanni Guerrini and Giorgio Quaroni, the representatives of the Sindacato fascista Belle Arti (Union of artists fascist fine arts) were asked to run the artistic project. Many initiatives were planned around the Exposition in a way typical for colonial and other large exhibitions. For instance, international conferences on the theme of the colonies, colonial art exhibitions and retrospectives of colonial art were held and a zoo with African fauna and a tropical aquarium was built here.

The influences of the official propaganda on the exhibition design and content were visible around the entire exhibition ground. The exhibition was organized in three sectors – historical, geographical and manufacture. 36 permanent pavilions were built here as showrooms alongside three theatres, two restaurants, an Olympic-size swimming pool, botanical greenhouses as well as an entertainment park. The Exhibition was attended by representatives from the Italian colonies not only in Africa but also from Albania or the Greek islands of the Dodecanese, and the most powerful European countries were also invited to visit. The international outreach was evident from the range of exhibitions guides which were available in English, French, German and Spanish.

Three specific typologies of the exhibition sections can be detected in the *Triennale*. The first section was an exhibition dedicated to the cult of Roman civilization, characterized by a dual propagandistic objective: the glorification of the Roman Empire, in close relationship with the foundation of the new Italian Empire, and the epic fascist conquest of overseas territories. The archaeological findings from the ancient Roman conquests in Africa displayed here were used as a link between the colonial past and present.

The second type is related to the fact that colonial exhibitions were characterized by the overall eclecticism of the collections on display: the memories and photographs of explorers, weapons and local products or artefacts were all selected and exposed with the purpose of demonstrating the wealth of the conquered territories, as well as the existence of new territories, ready to be conquered by Mussolini's new Italy. The core part of these exhibits were pictures and photo-mosaics, which not only covered entire walls of the pavilions, but were incorporated into the architecture, thus becoming an integral part of the exhibition design. The geographical section contained anthropological and ethnographic documentation: each exposition was intended to show the life of the different regions of the

Empire, from Africa to Albania and the Dodecanese Islands. Within each territorial partition, the variety of the social and material life was deployed. As in earlier colonial exhibitions, natives, craft shops, reproductions of houses and public places evoking the atmosphere of Africa were an essential element. Such a simulation of scenes of African life had the intent to seduce visitors' emotions. A number of live shows were staged here not to document the actual complexity of relationships in daily-life, but to depict African countries as exotic lands and destinations for heroic deeds and adventures.

The third typology contained merchandise exhibits focused mainly on the production and work sectors and offered large wall decorations and unexpected space articulations, for example the spectacular layout of the Mostra dell'Elettrotecnica (the Show of Electrotechnics) realized by the Futurist artist Enrico Prampolini: he exhibited a lit model of the Italian peninsula, showing the potential of electricity production in Italy by a large illuminated spiral that started in the centre of the peninsula and led up to the ceiling. These exhibits, homed in permanent buildings divided into five sub-sectors, were meant to show both the economic situation of the

Italian colonies and examine their reinforcing role in the Italian national plan for self-sufficiency.

During the interwar period, Naples was historically and geographically disconnected from the current debates in the field of art and architecture. The *Triennale d'Oltremare* offered the city the chance to develop a unique concept of territorial planning, of the role of the city as well as on the ephemeral architecture and artistic features. The Exhibition was not only conceived as the finishing intervention into the urban district of Fuorigrotta but, mainly, as a future vision for the renewal of the whole city. The *Triennale* became the amplifying core of the function of Naples in relation to activities closely linked to the life of the empire: it was thought of as a real 'idea of the city' whose trade and touristic sectors where going to play a key role.

Architecture and art played a fundamental role in the *Triennale*, not only in the general project but also in the specific exposition choices, which were aimed at making the visit simple and enjoyable. The wide range of displays undertaken by the designers of the exhibitions, documented by a few fragments that have survived, became an exemplary model for future Italian exposition-design. The recurring subjects, such as imperial eagles, fasces, Roman archaeological fragments combined with the standard display apparatus, including large photomontages and written comments on the exhibited works, did not restrain some artists and architects from achieving high-quality exposition stands.

Propaganda campaigns of the thirties and forties in Italy were mainly based on several aesthetic tendencies: the first one was the model of the Exhibition of the Fascist Revolution (1932), inspired by the experimental futuristic art and implemented through the extensive use of photomontages and typographic techniques. The other tendency, introduced a little later, was inspired by rationalism and was promoted by those artists and architects that worked at the Milan Triennial Expositions including Edoardo Persico, Marcello Nizzoli, Giuseppe Terragni and Giuseppe Pagano, a group of modernist architects who embraced the international architectural language.

The *Triennale d'Oltremare*, too, was designed and built using the model of the 1932 Exhibition of the Fascist Revolution, which was held in Rome to commemorate the first ten years of the Fascist government. Many young architects and artists took part in the preparation and devised new models of construction in Naples. A thematic exhibition was subdivided into several sections, each devoted to a particular aspect of the Exposition theme, covering the main stages in the history of the Fascist government from its birth to the regime's rise to power. From the outset, the exhibition was conceived not as an objective representation of the facts, based solely exposure of historical documents, but as a celebratory work and propaganda that was to influence and emotionally engage visitors. For this reason, in addition to historical figures such as Dino Alfieri and Luigi Freddi were called to cooperate exponents of various artistic movements of the time including Mario Sironi, Enrico Prampolini, Gerardo Dottori, Adalberto Libera and Giuseppe Terragni.

In an attempt to validate Italy’s position in Europe and in the world, the *Triennale d’Oltremare* also made a recurrent comparison between the history before the colonial conquest and the colonial situation. Factual data, photomontages and decorative panels were used to show simulations of production and the effects of ‘modernizers’ on the traditional technologies. In comparison, approach to colonial objects at previous expositions was simpler and similar to the fairs in Tripoli, where exhibits consisted only of commercial products from the colonies without any graphic and photographic support.

The variety of exhibits on show at the Naples *Triennale*, both of a colonialist formulation and produced according to the logic of 'spectacular' modernist settings and organized following the experimental techniques of the Futuristic movement, were not far away from the typical 'propaganda aesthetics'. Such aesthetics was characterized by the use of all possible visual instruments, photographic and artistic and was intended for the dissemination of Fascist myths as well as for education of the masses. In these particular cases exhibits were aimed at the exaltation of the myth of the Empire and of the colonial conquest. In such a context the exhibits were converted into purely symbolic elements capable of producing emotional reactions; the visitor was flooded by successive waves of environmental reconstructions, images, documents, photographs of the Italian colonies, stylized silhouettes, models, sculptures, murals, giant and mosaic photographs recalling places, events and protagonists of the colonial achievements. Significant in this respect was the Tower of P.N.F., a 46 m high 'symbol' of the regime which dominated the entire complex. A decorative frieze with a bas-relief, designed by Pasquale Meconio and Vincenzo Monaco, completely encircled the base of the tower and depicted the exploits of Mussolini's Legionaries in a reference to those of the legionaries of Rome. The theme of 'colonial conquests' of the regime was thus emphasized by the frieze and completed with a giant sculpture of the Victorious Fascist on the west elevation, covered with slabs of travertine by the same designers.

The *Triennale d'Oltremare* developed its own brand of strong symbolic and evocative imagery, which perhaps exceeded the value of the architecture itself. Conceived in a historical context in which every creative act has to be a political gesture, its primary aim was to impress the observer through its visual impact and seductive impression. The arts were organically integrated into the architectural constructions as an essential contribution to most of the features. The exhibition's project involved both the *architetti integrali* (full-architects) coming from the most prestigious Italian schools and members of the 'Sarfatti movement', an artistic movement of the so-called 'return to order' which embraced classical art. Roman and Neapolitan artists, including the Futurists, Franco Girosi, Edgardo Mannucci, Paolo Ricci, Nicola Fabbricatore, Pietro Barillà and Tommaso Cascella were also represented.

For this reason the main contribution of the *Mostra d'Oltremare* was not only the intrinsic architectural quality of the buildings. As one of the largest exhibitions in Europe, it also had a vital role in contemporary art and culture. To support the commemorative program, historical documentation on a variety of topics together with works of art, situated outside and inside the buildings and pavilions, provided symbolic or illustrative visual atmosphere. The arts were organically integrated into architectural constructions, defining their peculiar characteristics. In the *Triennale d'Oltremare* in 1940, the original quest for balance between architectural structures and works of art emerged and give birth in some cases to a style characterized by a creative spontaneity. The decorative part of the pavilions informed of their exhibition content that aspect was well cared and artists and architects worked together.

About 120 artists, including Enrico Prampolini, Melkiorre Melis, Giovanni Brancaccio, Giulio Rosso, Alberto Chiancone, were invited to collaborate in the production of the artistic decoration of the exhibition. An impressive repertoire of sculptures, wall paintings, large mosaics, interior decorations, ceramic carpets and panels was created and although almost completely destroyed shortly after the exhibition's closure, it however made a strong artistic imprint of a great open air art exhibition. Only a few works of this big project have survived as most of it fell victim to the bombing by American and retreating German troops during the Second World War.

The simultaneous use of the 'sisters arts' complemented the role of architecture. The whole artistic project was the core of the event and could be considered as an emblematic episode of that period, in which the government experimented with the ambitious path towards a social and political art through the use of Mario Sironi's 'great decorations.' In the period between 1920 and 1940 the official Italian cultural orientation attempts to overcome individualistic aesthetics of the avant-garde and gives art a social function of communication and collective education. In particular, the use of mural painting, the communicative power of which was considered crucial for popular masses, was theorized in 1933 by Sironi. He drafted the Manifesto of Mural Painting with contributions from the artists Massimo Campigli, Carlo Carrà and Achille Funi, in which he asserted that mural painting was a quintessentially social phenomenon that operated on the popular imagination more than any other form of painting.

In the *Triennale d'Oltremare*, the governmental patronage of public art allowed artists who both were and were not members of the *Sindacato*

Fascista di Belle Arti (the Fascist Fine Arts Union) to participate in the development of the visual image of the Exhibition. The architect and painter Charles Cocchia, for instance, designed a restaurant with a swimming pool as a successful integration between architecture and decoration. The ceramic decorations produced at the factory Posillipo in Naples played a crucial role in giving character to the interior of the restaurant. Interior and exterior ceramic decorations of other buildings and pavilions also used traditional craftsmanship and confirmed its compatibility with the modern setting. And because at previous exhibitions the regime officials had never given space to rationalist architecture, the close relationship between art and architecture comes across as one of the most significant and original contribution of the *Mostra*.

Another example of such interaction is Pavilion Libya, designed by Florestano di Fausto. Its *Caffe Arabo,* however, also represents an interesting case study for a different reason, as it demonstrates the Italian relation to its colony in an exhibition setting. The pavilion was divided into three areas, historical-geographical, ethnographic-documentary, and activities related to the metropolis and the regime in Libya. The decorative design of the *Caffè Arabo*, one of the most evocative of the Pavilion Libya was created by the artist Melkiorre Melis, who was responsible for the Italian School of Arts and Crafts of Tripoli. Melis was appointed to the role of painter, builder and decorator and held the position of artistic advisor at the Triennale.

The café therefore demonstrated the special role that the arts, ranging from painting and sculpture to interior decoration, held in the show. Melkiorre Melis worked in collaboration with the architect di Florestano di Fausto and the Pavilion Libya was presented to visitors as a composition of architectural volumes with a strong visionary character, in which local African models and decorative motifs Africans are processed in an original way. The architecture of the pavilion was reminiscent of Libyan cupolas and minarets, although their colour white turned them more into an idealized vision of such buildings.

Melis created numerous decorative projects for the *Triennale*, among which were three large designs for majolica tiles for the exhibition of ceramics in the Pavilion Libya and a design of a tondo with gazelles for a large ceramic panel of 2.6 meters for the *Caffè Arabo* of the Pavilion Libya. In the Pavilion, Melis continued his experimenting with fine art and applied art and created decorative panels for the entrance to the pavilion. It was reminiscent of his previous work for the School of Arts and Crafts of Tripoli and for a Moorish café in the pavilion Libya, which was reconstructed using a model of a café located in the ancient district of Souk el Muscir in Tripoli. In the design of the Moorish café, Melis was inspired by the colourful and dynamic paintings and photographs he made in Libya. He selected recurring patterns of gazelles on the run, Arab-Egyptian dances, cypress decorations with animals and nature as well as numerous ornaments such as purely decorative arabesques which were used by local artists. Melis did not design just the ceramics but also decorative furniture with the aim of turning the café into a universal work of art. It is possible to reconstruct, at least in part, the physiognomy of the Moorish café from the photographic documentation of the inauguration of the *Triennale* and from the sketches of some of the ceramic panels. The walls were decorated with round ceramics that were freely inspired by the geometric patterns designed by Melis for the realization of brass plates and embossed copper. The entrance doors were also decorated with ceramic tiles in geometric patterns. A ceramic floor (7.20 x 3.20 meters), consisting of a decorative motive in racemes twisted cypresses which surrounded an area for a small music band and Arabic dancers. The whole room was furnished with tables and chairs with simple design reminiscent of an unspecified oriental style by which Melis created a real brand of Moorish café. Its most characteristic feature consisted of a motive of a six-pointed star and a moon blade, which was placed on the tables, on chairs, on the walls.

With his artistic production inspired by Libyan local craft, Melis directly fitted the eclectic decorative and colonial project of the *Triennale*. After five years spent in Libya's Muslim School of Arts and Crafts and the School of Artisan Ceramics, Melis was able to design ceramics, decorative furniture, pitchers and plates in a uniform style in order to create a global artistic product.

Within the confines of the *Triennale*, the original and innovative development of the dialectical relationship between architecture and ceramic decoration satisfied the communicative and functional aspect and influenced artistic expression and the promotion of material design. Because of Italy's entrance in the Second World War, the *Triennale* closed less than a month after its opening, suffering in the subsequent years many damages due to the incessant bombings over the city of Naples. The two bombardments in August 1943 seriously affected the area of the Exhibition. In the ambiguous position that ranged from war booty and occupied zone, the fate of the *Triennale d'oltremare* may be counted among the inevitable tolls of war.

The function and focus of the exhibition complex in Naples had been defined since its creation: its duration, the public, the spectacular combination of educational and recreational purposes, the scope and logic of a route that would make the content readable and understandable, it was a matter of pride for the citizens of Naples to express in that ephemeral event the dream of the colonialist drive, that it was to recreate every three years, becoming progressively an open-air museum. The decision to overcome the limits and the frontier of a single building in the exhibition which distinguished it from the two previous international colonial art exhibitions at Rome in 1931 and Naples in 1934-1935, was a clear and spectacular statement of intent. The exhibition was conceived from the beginning as a big park and the city centre, in strict relationship with the landscape and was defined as the original experience of the Fascist period in Italy. The policy of Fascism in the first half of the twentieth century aimed to connote territories and cities with a 'special presence'. This included streets, squares, buildings, as well as exhibition spaces, and the *Triennale d'Oltremare* can be considered one of these special presences. The Triennale today documents an important era in Italian history characterized by an intense cultural activity related to its colonies and territorial and cultural expansion. The works of art, architecture, sculpture from the Italian colonies, but also those created specially for the event, represent an important integration between art and propaganda together with the strategy of involving the masses on the grounds of an exhibition.

Per un approfondimento sul progetto architettonico, i padiglioni, le opere d'arte, gli allestimenti espositivi della Triennale d'Oltremare di Napoli del 1940 si veda G. Arena, *Visioni d'oltremare. Allestimenti e politica dell'immagine nelle esposizioni coloniali del XX secolo*, Napoli 2011 e G. Arena, *Napoli 1940-1952, dalla Prima Mostra Triennale delle Terre Italiane d'Oltremare alla Prima Mostra Triennale del lavoro italiano nel mondo*, Napoli 2012.

La città 6 dell'E42

Esporre il Primato italiano

Le ultime realizzazioni espositive del regime, la manifestazione coloniale italiana di Napoli *Prima Mostra Triennale delle terre italiane d'Oltremare,* (inaugurata il 9 maggio 1940) e l'Esposizione Universale di Roma indicata sin dalla sua ideazione con la sigla E42,[1] approvata dal Bureau International nel giugno del 1936 e mai inaugurata[2], mostrano alcuni significativi punti di incontro nelle tematiche adottate: potenza imperiale, primato italiano, *mare nostrum*, archeologia[3].

Le due Esposizioni avrebbero dovuto mostrare agli italiani e all'estero i traguardi raggiunti dal regime e mostrare una nuova tipologia di spazio pubblico, dove architetture ed opere d'arte, avrebbero dovuto diffondere ed enfatizzare l'immagine di potenza del regime.

La Mostra d'Oltremare avrebbe dovuto documentare, la natura dell'intervento italiano in Etiopia, precedente e successivo alla conquista, il

---

1 *E42* è la sigla ufficiale di questa Esposizione, mentre la sigla *Eur*, con cui nel dopoguerra sarà chiamato il nuovo quartiere che si costruisce a partire dal 1937, deriva dalla legge che nel dicembre del 1936 istituisce l'Ente Autonomo incaricato di provvedere all'organizzazione e al funzionamento dell'Esposizione Universale di Roma.

2 L'idea dell'*E 42*, l'Esposizione Universale di Roma, prende forma nel 1935 da un progetto di Giuseppe Bottai. Su richiesta dell'Italia, il *Bureau International des Expositions*, nel giugno del 1936, accoglie la domanda dell'Italia di tenere in Roma nel 1942 una *Esposizione generale di prima categoria*. L'Esposizione avrebbe dovuto essere inaugurata in un primo momento nella ricorrenza del ventennale della Rivoluzione fascista: il 23 marzo 1942. Cfr. Lettera di Benito Mussolini a Giuseppe Bottai, Roma 23 giugno 1935-XIII, ACS, Segreteria particolare del duce, carteggio ordinario (SPDco), 1922-1943, b. 1268, copia dattiloscritta, 1 pagina.

3 La più ampia sistemazione urbanistica ipotizzata per l'E42, è ascrivibile al carattere universale che l'esposizione doveva rivestire, cfr. E. Gentile, *Fascismo di pietra*, Bari 2010.

cui possesso trasformava la piccola Italia dei primi anni del Novecento in un impero coloniale[4].

L'E42 adotterà un tema più vasto: "Olimpiadi della civiltà", seguito dal motto: "Ieri - oggi - domani". La formula sembra sintetizzare il destino di Roma: "*...Tutti i popoli, tutti i secoli, tutte le forme di attività...*"[5].

La razza, i costumi, gli usi, la religione, l'arte, la scienza, la tecnica, gli ordinamenti politici, sociali ed economici sarebbero compiutamente espressi nella formula "Olimpiadi della Civiltà", che preannunciava ed istituiva una gara, dalla quale l'Italia, nella visione del regime, avrebbe dovuto emergere[6].

L'Esposizione del 1942, veniva dopo una serie di tre manifestazioni consecutive a carattere internazionale e di grande rilievo: quella di Parigi del 1937[7], quella di New York del 1939, quella di Tokio del 1940 (non realizzata)[8]; dunque, nella rassegna comparativa delle conquiste civili di

---

[4] Nel fascismo, il mito dell'impero, come centro irradiatore di civiltà universale, non era un'improvvisazione propagandistica collegata alla conquista dell'Etiopia, ma presente fin dai primi tempi del movimento, ed emerse in modo più evidente, non solo attraverso il colonialismo, ma soprattutto attraverso la valorizzazione della funzione rivoluzionaria del fascismo come movimento universale e non soltanto italiano, che aspirava non solo all'espansione territoriale ma a diffondere nel mondo la forza di una nuova civiltà, cfr. G. De Matteis, *Verso l'equilibrio della nuova Europa*, Firenze 1941, pp. 160-161; G. Bottai, *Il problema della ricostruzione*, cit. in R. De Felice, *Autobiografia del fascismo*, Roma 1978, pp. 533-566; R. De Felice, *Mussolini il duce. Gli anni del consenso 1929-1936*, Torino 2006, pp. 758-808; E. Gentile, *Nuova civiltà imperiale*, in *La Grande Italia. Il mito della nazione del XX secolo*, Bari 2006, pp. 193-207.

[5] Cfr. *Commissariato Generale, Esposizione Universale di Roma, E 42. Programma di Massima, giugno XV*, ACS, SPDco, 1922-1943, b. 1268, dattiloscritto, 46 pagine.

[6] Cfr. Quivis, *L'Esposizione Universale di Roma*, in «Le Vie d'Italia», a. XLIV, n. 2, febbraio 1938, pp. 161-167.

[7] Sull'Esposizione Universale di Parigi del 1937 cfr. R. Zveteremic, *Prima visita all'Esposizione di Parigi*, in «Casabella», a.X, n. 115, luglio 1937, pp. 2-13.

[8] L'Esposizione di Parigi (duecentoquaranta padiglioni e quarantadue nazioni presenti) iniziata con un programma limitatissimo assunse poi, durante la fase esecutiva, notevoli dimensioni:

tutti i popoli, l'E42 aveva il compito di esprimere la potenza raggiunta dall'Italia imperiale e di affermare il suo valore in tutti i campi[9].

Ogni Esposizione internazionale si ispira ad un motivo o tema che serva da orientamento. Così ad esempio, quella di Chicago del 1933 si definì :"*Un secolo di progresso*"; quella di Parigi del 1937: "*Arti e Tecniche nella vita moderna*"; quella di New York del 1939: "*Per costruire il mondo di domani*"[10].

Il motivo soprattutto ideologico dell'Esposizione italiana del 1942, quello di Roma come centro di confluenza della civiltà universale, si concretizza nell'emblema dell'Esposizione stessa, l'aureo di Adriano, che fu poi ripetuto nel sesterzio di Antonio Pio. Sul verso di quella moneta appare per la prima volta il motto: "Roma Aeterna"[11].

La moneta offre dunque, nella figurazione e nel motto, l'ideale simbolo del destino di Roma unitamente al richiamo dell'Imperatore Adriano, cultore delle arti e delle scienze, e promotore di costruzioni monumentali.

Nel mese di gennaio del 1937 Mussolini, su proposta dei commissari per l'Esposizione universale di Roma (il senatore Vittorio Cini e gli onorevoli Cipriano Efisio Oppo e Oreste Bonomi) incaricava gli architetti Giuseppe Pagano, Marcello Piacentini, Luigi Piccinato, Ettore Rossi e Luigi Vietti di

---

l'Esposizione americana si estese su seicento ettari di superficie e costò oltre due miliardi e mezzo di lire; l'Esposizione giapponese doveva coincidere con le Olimpiadi, elemento quest'ultimo che ne aumentò, durante la fase di preparazione, la risonanza anche nel mondo occidentale.

[9] Cfr. *Pro=memoria per il Duce*, 30 giugno 1935-XIII, ACS, SPDco, 1922-1943, b. 1268, dattiloscritto, 2 pagine.

[10] Cfr. E. Godoli, *L'E 42 e le esposizioni universali*, in M. Calvesi, E. Guidoni, S. Lux, (a cura di), *E 42. Utopia e scenario del regime*, vol. II, *Urbanistica, architettura, arte e decorazione*, Venezia 1987, pp. 147-155; G. Lipovetsky, *L'impero dell'effimero*, Milano 1989.

[11] Cfr. L. Breglia, *Numismatica antica. Storia e metodologia* , 1967, tav. 42.

studiare il piano regolatore della grande Esposizione. Individuata, da parte del commissariato, la zona in cui dovrà sorgere l'esposizione e rilevato il terreno con il procedimento aerofotografico Nistri, gli architetti hanno successivamente studiato, nel mese di marzo, un primo progetto di massima. Nel mese di aprile veniva presentato al capo del governo un secondo progetto di massima che prevedeva una zona di estensione di 200 ettari, eventualmente ampliabile. Su questo progetto, approvato da Mussolini, veniva elaborato il progetto di massima definitivo, che nel giorno 28 aprile veniva confermato con un sopralluogo sulla zona individuata e con la simbolica piantagione di tre pini nell'area in cui sorgerà il palazzo della Civiltà italiana.

Inizialmente prevista in tre gruppi - Roma, Magnana, Lido - l'Esposizione fu poi ubicata nella zona presso l'Abbazia delle Tre Fontane, a circa due chilometri dalla Basilica di San Paolo, che confinava con il limite del piano regolatore di Roma del 1931.

Con questa scelta si mirava a creare non un complesso provvisorio e occasionale per l'effimera durata di una esposizione, ma la struttura stabile per un primo nuovo grande centro di Roma, proiettato verso il mare. Per questa ragione, infatti, gli architetti non si sono preoccupati soltanto dell'organizzazione degli spazi destinati ai padiglioni espositivi, ma hanno preparato gli studi per la futura evoluzione della zona. L'Esposizione del 1942 fu concepita dunque come creazione definitiva, come definitivo fu considerato lo stile architettonico ed artistico dell'era fascista *E42*, uno

stile caratterizzato da monumentalità ed astrazione delle forme[12].
L'aspetto più complesso e delicato del lavoro di preparazione fu indubbiamente quello logistico: strade, accessi, parchi, studio del paesaggio, edifici permanenti, padiglioni, progetto artistico, raggruppamento ed ordinamento delle mostre.
Si cercò di conciliare il criterio dell'ordinamento per nazioni con le possibilità e le opportunità di istituire mostre internazionali.
Per corrispondere inoltre a specifiche richieste di altri Stati fu prevista la costruzione di padiglioni provvisori destinati ad ospitare "mostre varie".
Ogni mostra doveva avere una sintetica premessa storica del progresso (ieri), una parte più ampia che illustrava i traguardi raggiunti (oggi) ed una terza parte destinata a proiettare uno sguardo sugli sviluppi futuri (domani).
Prescindendo dai raggruppamenti consuetudinari, l'Esposizione fu suddivisa in sezioni, attribuendo poi la qualifica di città ad ognuna delle sezioni, e di quartiere ad ognuno dei gruppi compresi nella città dell'Economia Corporativa.
Nella relazione sul progetto tecnico dell'E42 sono indicati i tre punti principali sui quali dovrà costruirsi la grandiosità del complesso, in primo luogo l'estensione della zona occupata al fine di superare gli spazi espositivi delle precedenti esposizioni di categoria, l'ordinamento edilizio e la realizzazione architettonica tale da costituire un episodio espositivo di

---

[12] La distinzione tra edifici definitivi e provvisori indusse a considerare l'opportunità di seguire procedure diverse di progettazione. Mentre per i padiglioni provvisori fu utilizzato il sistema dei concorsi pubblici, per la progettazione degli edifici a carattere permanente furono *invitati*, d'accordo con le organizzazioni sindacali di categoria, architetti ed artisti strettamente legati al regime, per un approfondimento si veda E. Gentile, *Fascismo di pietra*, Bari 2007.

"assoluta novità" e "rarità eccezionale" che possa "segnare una epoca di stile", quello dell'anno XX dell'era fascista, la presentazione efficiente e definitiva del Corporativismo Fascista[13].

Dal programma di massima del 1937[14] si legge che le sezioni dovevano essere sette:

1. *città Italiana*, raggruppamento degli edifici e delle mostre a carattere nazionale, che non appartengono ad altre mostre specifiche;
2. *città delle Nazioni*, raggruppamento del contributo internazionale all'Esposizione;
3. *città dell'Arte*, raggruppamento delle mostre di pittura, scultura, architettura, poesia, e musica;
4. *città della Scienza*, raggruppamento delle mostre per il "Progresso scientifico universale";
5. *città dell'Economia Corporativa*, interamente italiana, avrebbe dovuto offrire una convincente visione del sistema economico instaurato dal fascismo;
6. *città dell'Africa Italiana*, una grande mostra coloniale;
7. *città degli svaghi.*

Sebbene non compresa nella zona di competenza dell'Esposizione, fu prevista nel programma generale la sistemazione di Ostia antica, con un ampliamento degli scavi, con il ripristino del teatro romano per gli

---

[13] Cfr. *Progetto di massima per una Esposizione Universale a Roma, 23 marzo 1939 o 1942,* ACS, SPDco, 1922-1943, b. 1268, dattiloscritto di 10 pagine.

[14] Cfr. *Commissariato Generale, Esposizione Universale di Roma, E 42. Programma di massima, giugno XV*, ACS, SPDco, 1922-1943, b. 1268, dattiloscritto, 46 pagine.

spettacoli classici, con la costruzione di un edificio per una mostra archeologica con destinazione successiva a museo.

Nel programma di massima dell'E42 alla voce "Sezione VI – Città dell'Africa Italiana" si legge: "*In un gruppo di Padiglioni caratteristici verrà sviluppata la grande Mostra Coloniale. Sarà illustrata e documentata la creazione dell'Impero Italiano; dai pionieri che hanno legato il loro nome alla scoperta e alla valorizzazione delle terre di oltre mare, sino all'ultima conquista in A.O.*

Sarà utilizzata l'esperienza preziosa delle precedenti Esposizioni Coloniali. Saranno portati a Roma i cimeli, i ricordi, il materiale necessario a rendere memorando l'anno nel quale, con l'Esposizione di Roma, si celebrerà il primo quinquennio dell'Impero.

La flora, la fauna, la produzione indigena, gli usi, i costumi, le risorse minerali, idriche, agricole delle terre italiane d'Africa; la documentazione delle varie fasi di conquista e valorizzazione dell'Impero: insomma tutto ciò che può mettere in luce, documentare e potenziare l'azione del Governo Fascista, sarà rappresentato in modo organico, completo e suggestivo"[15].

A leggere attentamente è qui riproposto, in sintesi, il programma della I Mostra Triennale delle Terre Italiane d'Oltremare[16] ed il riferimento alle "Precedenti Esposizioni Coloniali" indica un richiamo evidente alla Triennale di Napoli.

---

[15] *Commissariato Generale, Esposizione Universale di Roma, E 42. Programma di Massima*, ACS, SPDco , 1922-1943, dattiloscritto, pp. 38-39.

[16] Cfr. G. Arena, *Visioni d'Oltremare. Allestimenti e politica dell'immagine nelle esposizioni coloniali del XX secolo*, cit.

Nonostante il carattere tematico (coloniale) di ambito nazionale, per la realizzazione della Triennale d'Oltremare il regime scelse di adottare lo stesso *iter* progettuale che si stava seguendo per la World Exhibition E42[17], tale scelta conferma la vocazione internazionale della mostra partenopea. Anche lo sforzo propagandistico è paragonabile a quello dell'E42[18]: 50.000 cartelli di propaganda affissi in tutte le città d'Italia e d'oltremare, 1000 mq coperti con gigantografie pubblicitarie su strade e autostrade nazionali, 1000 cartelli metallizzati nelle stazioni delle Ferrovie dello Stato, 8000 cartellini sottovetro nelle carrozze dei treni, 500 vetrofanie, 4 grandi tabelloni luminosi di pubblicità a Roma e Milano, 9.000.000 di francobolli chiudi lettera, 150.000 pieghevoli in 4 lingue, 250.000 pieghevoli, 500.000 segnalibri, 100.000 cartoline dei luoghi della Triennale, 80.000 cartellini di propaganda nei negozi, note e pubblicità sulla stampa nazionale ed internazionale[19], comunicazioni e conferenze radio, documentari LUCE[20],

---

[17] Il termine *World Exibition* indica una *Esposizione Internazionale Registrata*, comunemente nota come *Esposizione Universale*. L'organismo internazionale che regola la frequenza, la qualità e lo svolgimento delle esposizioni è il *Bureau International des Expositions* (BIE), nato da una convenzione internazionale siglata a Parigi nel 1928. Attualmente aderiscono al BIE 102 Stati, cfr. http://www.bie-paris.org, sito ufficiale del BIE.

[18] Sull'imponente campagna propagandistica del regime per l'E42 si veda *Ente Autonomo Esposizione Universale di Roma, Programma di massima per la propaganda E 42, Roma 10 marzo 1939*, Archivio Storico-Diplomatico del Ministero degli Affari Esteri (AMAE), fondo del Ministero della Cultura Popolare (MCP), Ministero stampa e propaganda (MSP), b. 190, dattiloscritto, 21 pagine.

[19] Questa la situazione registrata dagli uffici dell'Ente Mostra al 13 novembre 1939: 34.328 tra articoli, note e comunicati su quotidiani e settimanali, 35.514 tra note e pagine pubblicitarie su riviste tecniche e giornali e riviste esteri. Cfr. *Mostra Triennale delle Terre Italiane d'Oltremare. Stampa e Propaganda, situazione al 13 novembre 1939*, dattiloscritto in 2 pagine su carta intestata dell'Ente Autonomo Mostra Triennale delle Terre Italiane d'Oltremare. ASNA, GP, Secondo versamento, f. 879.

[20] Il Servizio propaganda dell'Ente Autonomo Triennale d'Oltremare e quello dell'Ente Autonomo E42 affidarono all'Istituto LUCE, il compito di documentare con fotografie e filmati l'intero processo di progettazione e costruzione delle due Esposizioni, la maggior parte dei

partecipazione con stands promozionali alla Fiera di Bari, di Milano e di Lipsia, e all'Esposizione Universale di New York[21].

Questa decisione e la martellante campagna di informazione dovevano consentire, nelle aspirazioni di Mussolini, di avvalersi di un duplice strumento propagandistico di portata internazionale negli anni dell'affermazione espansionistica italiana[22].

Per la messa in scena del potere a Roma, come a Napoli, furono utilizzati, non a caso, gli stessi strumenti di attuazione. Si trattava di procedure già collaudate per la fondazione di città nuove[23] realizzate dal regime: l'istituzione di un apposito Ente Autonomo, la dichiarazione di pubblica utilità per la realizzazione delle opere previste, la decretazione degli espropri necessari da effettuarsi in tempi brevi, la costituzione di un Commissariato autorizzato ad eseguire le espropriazioni dei terreni e condurre a termine tutti i lavori necessari alla costruzione degli edifici.

La scelta della capitale come sede della World Exhibition italiana del 1942 è scontata: portarice di una storia gloriosa e millenaria, luogo ideale della

---

filmati vennero girati per documentare le visite di personalità e soltanto alcuni riportano lo stato di avanzamento dei lavori. La documentazione dei due episodi è particolarmente significativa per l'analisi del rapporto architettura-propaganda.

[21] Cfr. *Mostra Triennale delle Terre Italiane d'Oltremare. Stampa e Propaganda, situazione al 13 novembre 1939*, dattiloscritto in 2 pagine su carta intestata dell'Ente Autonomo Mostra Triennale delle Terre Italiane d'Oltremare. ASNA, GP, Secondo versamento, f. 879.

[22] La simbiosi fra la riapparizione dell'impero e l'idea dell'esposizione, come realizzazione della nuova romanità fascista, fu decisiva per la concezione e la realizzazione dell'E42, dal punto di vista funzionale e soprattutto dal punto di vista simbolico. Cfr. E. Gentile, *Fascismo di pietra*, cit. pp. 183-190.

[23] Sulle città di fondazione si veda A. Dal Piaz, A. Mesolella, *L'urbanistica in Italia nel Novecento*, in «ArQ 12», *Architettura italiana 1920-1939*, giugno 1994, Napoli 1996, pp. 45-72.; G. Pagano, *Architettura e città durante il fascismo*, Roma-Bari 1976; V. Franchetti Pardo, a cura di, *L'architettura nelle città italiane del XX secolo, dagli anni Venti agli anni Ottanta*, Milano 2003.

sintesi e delle aspirazioni della civiltà contemporanea, doveva dimostrare il proprio primato, e con esso, il primato dell'era fascista di fronte al mondo intero[24].

"...L'esposizione universale di Roma vuole essere la consacrazione dello sforzo che tutte le genti civili fanno sul cammino del progresso, non soltanto materiale. Ogni italiano deve intendersi personalmente impegnato. La parte italiana dell'E.42 è destinata a rimanere nei secoli, con edifici che avranno le proporzioni di S. Pietro e del Colosseo..."[25].

Il tema del primato italiano ritorna anche nella Triennale d'Oltremare e si riallaccia direttamente alle recenti conquiste coloniali.

Le tematiche del lavoro, della cultura, dell'arte, della scienza, anch'esse sviluppate nei tre settori della Mostra di Napoli, non servivano solamente ad esaltare l'impresa coloniale, considerata come l'ultimo atto di una serie storica iniziata con la conquista romana del bacino Mediterraneo africano

---

[24] Il fascismo si richiamava alla Roma imperiale, per il dominio mondiale che essa aveva attuato, ma guardava anche alla Roma repubblicana, come modello dell'identificazione del singolo con la vita dello Stato, e dunque come prefigurazione di una comunità totalitaria. La romanità evocata dal regime finiva così per amalgamare gli aspetti preferiti dell'una e dell'altra immagine, ricomponendo in sincronia alcuni caratteri, cronologicamente sfasati, della storia romana: il rigore morale del cittadino repubblicano e il potere del principe, l'austera sintesi della nazione e il fascino del sistema imperiale nella sua fase matura. Il richiamo alla romanità doveva anche qualificare una peculiare via di incontro con la modernità. La stessa conquista dell'Etiopia era vista insieme come "romana" e "modernissima", cfr. F. D'Amoja, *La politica estera dell'impero. Storia della politica estera fascista dalla conquista dell'Etiopia all'Anschluss*, Padova 1967; M. Cagnetta, *Antichisti e impero fascista*, Bari 1979; Ph. Cannistraro, *La fabbrica del consenso. Fascismo e mass media*, Roma-Bari 1975, p. 146; L. Canfora, *Ideologie del classicismo*, Torino 1980; AA.VV, *Fonti e problemi della politica coloniale italiana*, Atti del convegno, Taormina-Messina 23-29 ottobre 1989, Roma 1996; G. Belardelli, *Il mito fascista della romanità*, in *Il Ventennio degli intellettuali. Cultura, politica, ideologia nell'Italia fascista*, Bari 2005, pp. 206-236.

[25] *Discorso del Duce al rapporto per l'Esposizione Universale di Roma*, Agenzia Stefani, Roma 20 aprile 1939, n. 10, ore 12,43. Archivio Storico-Diplomatico del Ministero degli Affari Esteri, fondo del Ministero della Cultura Popolare, b. 190.

e del medio-oriente, consolidata poi dai successi commerciali delle repubbliche marinare e confermata con gli sviluppi della marineria italiana, ma soprattutto a testimoniare la differenza del dominio italiano nei confronti dei suoi possedimenti: non colonie di sfruttamento secondo il modello capitalistico, ma parti integranti della nazione, proiettate solo geograficamente lontano[26].

Le due Mostre quindi hanno il compito di esporre quel primato, concretizzarlo in opere stabili, renderlo spettacolarmente visibile.

Icone di Roma antica

Altri sono i temi ideali che segnano un punto di incontro tra le due Esposizioni: il *mare nostrum* e l'archeologia come ha già osservato Alessandra Muntoni .

Aver collocato l'E42 verso il mare aveva un significato insieme archeologico e imperiale: archeologico perché si radicava nelle origini marinare di Roma, e nella sussistenza che essa aveva tratto dal fiume Tevere[27]. Alla costruzione dell'immagine di Roma forte e vittoriosa sul mare si prodigò lo stesso Mussolini: "*...La storia Marittima di Roma antica, ci pone dinanzi*

---

[26] L. Preti, *Impero fascista, africani ed ebrei*, Milano, 1968.

[27] Cfr. *L'espansione dell'urbe verso il mare. Idee e proposte di S.E. Giovannoni sul progettato sviluppo urbanistico*, in «Il popolo di Roma», Roma, 24 ottobre 1936.

questi punti interrogativi: Roma antica fu anche brillante sul mare? Roma fu anche una grande potenza marinara? L'Impero di Roma fu anche marittimo? Rispondo affermativamente a questi punti interrogativi. Roma fu anche una grande potenza marinara. Senza il dominio del mare Roma non avrebbe conquistato, né potuto conservare l'Impero, perché molti popoli dovettero essere soggiogati per via di mare e a molti popoli conquistati, Roma più rapidamente poteva giungere per via di mare..."[28].

Il mito di Roma aveva aiutato il fascismo nella sua non facile ricerca d'identità, contrassegnando sin dall'inizio, e in un certo modo giustificando la sua vocazione all'espansione e alla conquista[29].

Non è un caso quindi, che negli stessi anni in cui si progettava l'Esposizione romana, gli scavi di Ostia Antica, iniziati e proseguiti per più di venti anni, vengono rilanciati come testimonianza dell'incontro ideale tra la moderna e l'antica civiltà di Roma. Quasi tutta la città antica è riportata alla luce, mentre si progetta ad Ostia un museo che avrebbe dovuto ospitare il materiale statuario ritrovato[30].

---

[28] B. Mussolini, *Roma antica sul mare*, Mantova 1929, p. 1.

[29] Il mito della missione di Roma nel mondo, sviluppato così ampiamente dal fascismo, era stato agitato già dal nazionalismo dell'Italia liberale in occasione delle "avventure" africane; appunto in nome dell'eredità politica e culturale di Roma si erano coltivati sogni di primato; oltre che la propaganda, anche la storiografia di ispirazione nazionalista aveva tentato un'identificazione della storia di Roma con la storia d'Italia, facendo uso di concetti e di un linguaggio del tutto analoghi a quelli che sarebbero stati poi tipici in età fascista, cfr. M. Cagnetta, *Il mito di Augusto e la "rivoluzione" fascista*, in «Quaderni di Storia», a. II, n. 3, gennaio-giugno 1976, pp. 139-181; L. Canfora, *Classicismo e fascismo, ibidem*, pp. 15-48; M. Isneghi, *L'educazione dell'italiano: il fascismo e l'organizzazione della cultura*, Bologna 1979; D. Veneruso, *L'Italia fascista. 1922-1945*, Bologna 1980; U. Alfassio Grimaldi, M. Addis Saba, *Cultura a passo romano: storia e strategie dei Littoriali della cultura e dell'arte*, Milano 1983.

[30] Cfr. G. Calza, *Ostia risorge per l'Esposizione Universale di Roma*, in «Le vie d'Italia» A. XLV, n. 9, settembre 1939, pp. 1228-1237.

L'E42, doveva ricordare le antiche tradizioni di conquista della città di Roma.
Spetta però alla Triennale d'Oltremare l'amplificazione di questo tema; il regime dispiega a Napoli, porto dell'impero italiano, una struttura che con i suoi padiglioni e le sue ricostruzioni ambientali, doveva illustrare il processo di colonizzazione italiana del Mediterraneo.
Anche alla Triennale d'Oltremare, si fa uso propagandistico dell'archeologia, cui viene dedicato un settore che viene collegato nel progetto architettonico alle attrazioni per il pubblico. Si tratta di vestigia rinvenute nel settore settentrionale della Mostra: tratti della Via Puteolana, un mausoleo in tufo con pilastri in laterizio e capitelli e cornici in cotto, un ramo dell'acquedotto romano del Serino.
L'archeologia, in entrambe le esposizioni giocò un ruolo importante come supporto propagandistico; quei ritrovamenti archeologici furono la dimostrazione concreta di continuità storica, politica ed artistica tra l'impero romano ed il regime fascista, non a caso per il manifesto della Triennale d'Oltremare, fu utilizzata una immagine ispirata alla romanità, ideata da Ugo Giammusso e Corrado Mancioli, divenuta un logo famosissimo, utilizzato per la copertina del catalogo, per le piccole guide all'esposizione, per depliant, volantini pubblicitari e piastrelle ricordo in ceramica[31]. Foto

---

[31] L'Archivio storico-architettonico della Mostra d'Oltremare (AMDO) conserva numerosi esemplari di questa produzione editoriale e pubblicitaria mentre la Collezione Wolfson di Genova (WG) conserva un esemplare della piastrella ricordo in ceramica, GD1990.574.1, prodotto dalla manifattura S.P.I.C.A. di Albisola (GE). Cfr. M. Fochessati, *Il senso del passato*, in S. Barisione, M. Fochessati, G. Franzone (a cura di), *La visione del prisma*, cit., p. 44.

La raffigurazione delle gambe di un soldato romano in marcia su di una strada lastricata romana riassumeva lo spirito dell'esposizione.

La prospettiva di collegamento tra le due ere imperiali fu chiaramente esplicitata nell'introduzione al catalogo nella Triennale: "*...La documentazione ampia e totalitaria dell'inesauribile forza di espansione della stirpe italiana nei secoli, la costante e feconda universalità del suo lavoro rappresenta di questa rassegna imperiale lo scopo politico maggiore. Tutto ciò che nei secoli è stato compiuto, ogni contributo di sangue e di pensiero, di fede e di volontà alla buona causa della civiltà romana, trova nella Triennale d'Oltremare la sua appassionata e fedele rievocazione, secondo un piano organico che ha per suprema ambizione .quella di presentare – offrendone non soltanto gli elementi dimostrativi ma soprattutto il senso – la continuità storica e ideale dell'idea imperiale di Roma, da Cesare a Mussolini...*"[32].

Questo modello di adesione a un progetto politico, basato su una vocazione imperialistica che si faceva discendere dalla tradizione romana, fu utilizzato anche nell'E42, ma nelle vicende dell'Esposizione Universale di Roma, gravava pure quel rapporto di competitività e, insieme di forzato adeguamento che contraddistingue le relazioni tra Italia e Germania in quegli anni. Ciò occorre in tutti i campi; dalla politica generale alla persecuzione antiebraica all'autarchia, fino ai problemi dello stile urbanistico. Il legame tra i due paesi, sancito poi dalla visita di Hitler a

---

[32] Cfr. *Prima Mostra Triennale delle Terre Italiane d'Oltremare. Napoli – Campi Flegrei, 9 maggio – 15 ottobre 1940-XVIII. Documentario*, Napoli 1940, p 10.

Roma (1938), presenta già nel 1936 profondi e variegati aspetti che investono tutti i campi della cultura[33].

Il rapporto esplicitato o sottaciuto, tra Italia e Germania investe, in primo luogo, il problema dell'Olimpiadi. Nel 1936 i giochi di Berlino sanciscono, di fronte al mondo, una superiorità tedesca che esercita, anche grazie all'apparato scenografico propagandistico, una grande influenza sull'opinione pubblica. Così l'Italia chiede di ospitare a sua volta i giochi: dopo Helsinki (1940) si prenota per il 1944. Una città olimpica doveva sorgere a Ostia, e di questa prospettiva, che già nella direzione di un ulteriore potenziamento del rapporto tra Roma e il mare, si tiene conto nelle prime proposte relative all'ubicazione dell'Esposizione, nell'ottobre del 1936. Ma l'idea dell'Olimpiade entra direttamente nel programma politico e culturale dell'esposizione, coniugandosi all'idea di civiltà. Lo scopo è, innanzi tutto di dimostrare la superiorità storica, artistica, scientifica e politica dell'Italia nei confronti della Germania, in un campo dove la vittoria sembra possibile[34].

Il progetto italiano delle Olimpiadi della Civiltà nasce nel clima imperiale dell'impresa etiopica. Al momento della proclamazione dell'impero, Mussolini sottolinea due aspetti, che ritorneranno frequentemente in molti altri discorsi: l'Italia vuole un "Impero di pace" e un "Impero di civiltà": *"...L'Italia ha finalmente il suo Impero...Impero di pace, perché*

---

[33] Cfr. I. Kershaw, *Hitler e l'enigma del consenso*, Roma-Bari 2006; V. Vidotto, *Hitler e il nazismo*, in AA.VV., *I volti del potere*, Roma-Bari 2010, pp. 219-247.

[34] B. M. Novarese, *L'effetto propagandistico delle Olimpiadi di Berlino del 1936 in Francia, Inghilterra, Italia e Stati Uniti*, tesi di laurea in Storia Contemporanea, Università degli Studi di Bologna, Facoltà di Lingue e Letterature straniere, a.a. 2002/2003, di cui una copia è conservata presso la Biblioteca del Museo Civico del Risorgimento di Bologna.

l'Italia vuole la pace per sé e per tutti e si decide alla guerra soltanto quando vi è forzata da impietosire, incoercibili necessità di vita. Impero di civiltà e di umanità per tutte le popolazioni dell'Etiopia...levate in alto, o legionari, le insegne, il ferro e i cuori, a salutare, dopo quindici secoli, la riapparizione dell'Impero sui colli fatali di Roma..."[35].

In questo clima generale, il 25 giugno 1936, quarantacinque giorni dopo la proclamazione dell'impero e venti giorni prima della revoca delle sanzioni[36], il *Buerau Internationale des Expositions* vota all'unanimità la risoluzione di riservare all'Italia il 1941 per la realizzazione di un'Esposizione Internazionale di prima categoria accogliendo così una richiesta avanzata fin dal novembre 1935[37].

La data del 1941 è definita dalle scadenze stabilite per queste Esposizioni: ogni sei anni. Quella data 1941, si incrocia con un'altra, il 1942, alla quale Mussolini ha pensato per un'esposizione universale da tenersi a Roma in occasione del ventennale del fascismo. Una volta ottenuta l'esposizione,

---

[35] B. Mussolini, *La proclamazione dell'Impero*, in «Il Popolo d'Italia», 10 maggio 1936; ora in *Opera Omnia di Benito Mussolini*, a cura di E. e D. Susmel, Firenze 1957, vol. XXVII, pp. 268-269.

[36] Le sanzioni economiche contro l'Italia, decretate dalla Società delle Nazioni il 18 novembre 1935 in seguito all'invasione dell'Etiopia, vengono revocate il 15 luglio 1936. In realtà, questa revoca ha carattere poco più che formale, in quanto di fatto le sanzioni sono state largamente disattese dagli stessi paesi che le hanno formulate (la Germania si è rifiutata di applicarle). Tuttavia, le sanzioni vengono sfruttate dal fascismo sia politicamente, creando l'immagine di un paese assediato dalle altre nazioni proprio perché avviato a divenire una potenza imperiale, sia economicamente, dando largo spazio a un regime autarchico, inteso come politica di protezione doganale a sostegno dei prezzi interni, secondo un modello adottato da moltissimi paesi in seguito alla crisi del 1929.

[37] Per un approfondimento sulle vicende relative all'assegnazione all'Italia della Esposizione Universale di Roma ed al progetto espositivo per il 1942 presentato da Bottai ed in seguito attribuito a Mussolini cfr. I. Insolera e L. Di Majo, *L'Eur e Roma dagli anni trenta al Duemila*, Roma-Bari 1986, pp. 8-11; E. Guidoni, *L'E 42, città della rappresentazione. Il progetto urbanistico e le polemiche sull'architettura*, in M. Calvesi, E. Guidoni, S. Lux, (a cura di), *E 42. Utopia e scenario del regime*, cit., vol. II, pp. 19-20.

essa comincia a essere presentata in Italia come l'«Esposizione del 1941-42», per poi divenire nei primi mesi del 1937 l'«Esposizione del 1942», l'«E42».

Il 26 dicembre 1936 entra in vigore la legge n. 2174 istitutiva dell'Ente Autonomo incaricato di organizzare l'Esposizione. Un successivo D.L. del 4 giugno 1938 ne stabilirà definitivamente la durata a partire dal 21 aprile 1942, per un periodo di sei mesi[38]. L'Ente dipenderà direttamente dal capo del governo ed avrà personalità giuridica propria. La rappresentanza dell'Ente è invece affidata ad un Commissariato presieduto da un commissario generale dell'Esposizione che Mussolini nomina nella persona di Vittorio Cini e da due commissari aggiunti: l'on. Bonomi, direttore generale del Turismo presso il ministero della Stampa e la propaganda, e l'on. Oppo, segretario generale della Quadriennale di Roma.

L'art. 13 della Legge istitutiva prevedeva che l'Ente, espletati i compiti per i quali era stato costituito, venisse liquidato con decreto del capo del governo. In realtà, l'Ente, non sarà mai posto in liquidazione ma, con finalità diverse da quella dell'Esposizione Universale procederà alla trasformazione degli spazi destinati allo svolgimento di eventi, manifestazioni e mostre in un quartiere residenziale.

Per trovare la disponibilità dei terreni necessari sarà usato lo strumento dell'espropriazione.

Nel gennaio del 1937 Mussolini incarica una Commissione urbanistica di redigere un progetto di piano regolatore di massima dell'Esposizione. I

---

[38] Anche in questo caso appare evidente la coincidenza con la durata della *Triennale d'Oltremare*, sei mesi anche per l'esposizione partenopea che doveva svolgersi dal 9 maggio al 15 ottobre del 1940.

componenti sono Giuseppe Pagano, Marcello Piacentini, Luigi Piccinato (impegnato con molteplici incarichi anche per la Triennale d'Oltremare di Napoli), Ettore Rossi, Luigi Vietti, il presidente è Oppo.

Il primo progetto è del 1937 ed è approvato da Mussolini l'8 aprile dello stesso anno. Contiene già alcuni degli elementi fondamentali che caratterizzeranno l'EUR; la via Imperiale, il lago, le piazze, il Palazzo della Civiltà ed il Palazzo dei Congressi, la chiesa, l'area per il quartiere residenziale[39].

Nel giugno del 1937, contemporaneamente alle prime espropriazioni, sono indetti i concorsi per la costruzione del Palazzo dei Ricevimenti e dei Congressi, e del Palazzo della Civiltà. Originariamente la costruzione dei padiglioni provvisori, destinati all'Esposizione, doveva avvenire tramite concorsi, mentre l'edificazione delle opere permanenti doveva avvenire tramite incarichi diretti ad accademici. Poi la parte provvisoria non si realizzerà, ma i concorsi saranno banditi per le opere definitive[40].

Il secondo progetto di piano, del marzo 1938, elaborato da Marcello Piacentini, è diverso dal precedente e presenta gli elementi in base ai quali

---

[39] Cfr. *Il Piano regolatore dell'Esposizione Universale di Roma 1941-1942 (architetti G. Pagano, M. Piacentini, L. Piccinato, E. Rossi, L. Vietti)*, in «Casabella», a. X, n. 114, giugno 1937, pp. 4-15; F. Bucci, S. Sala, *E42, Giuseppe Pagano - un progetto ritrovato*, in «Casabella», n. 842, ottobre 2014, pp. 6-37.

[40] Un primo progetto di massima, presentato (da Piacentini affiancato da Pagano, Piccinato, Vietti, Rossi) già all'inizio del 1937, per una «città» di concezione estremamente moderna sia per il linguaggio formale sia per l'uso dei materiali, acciaio, vetro, cemento, fu poi radicalmente modificato da Piacentini quando, in qualità di Preside della Facoltà di architettura di Roma, approntò, insieme al commissario dell'esposizione, i bandi di concorso per gli edifici «permanenti», nei quali si richiedevano espressioni architettoniche ispirate alla monumentalità, al classico, ai criteri della romanità. Cfr. G. Ciucci, *Una prima conclusione: l'E42*, in *Gli architetti e il fascismo*, cit., pp. 176-196; M. Mulazzani, *Roma E 42-XX. Programmi per un'Esposizione* in «Casabella», n. 842, ottobre 2014, pp. 38-41.

sarà costruito l'Eur come si presenta oggi. Cardodecumanico per eccellenza, il piano rielaborato da Piacentini ha la sua radice storica ed etimologica nelle città antiche di fondazione romana[41]: sull'asse principale della Via Imperiale si innestano ortogonalmente una serie di strade al termine delle quali sono collocati, come fondali, i palazzi.

Il terzo progetto, quello definitivo del 1939, è redatto dall'Ufficio Tecnico dell'Ente. In questo caso non vi sono rilevanti differenze con il progetto precedente. Tra la fine del 1938 e l'inizio del 1939 vengono appaltati i lavori e comincia la realizzazione dell'Esposizione.

Nelle intenzioni del regime e del comitato organizzatore l'insieme delle mostre, delle manifestazioni, delle iniziative e delle varie attività previste nell'ambito dell'E42 avrebbe dovuto valorizzare e promuovere tutte le "Attività creatrici dello spirito umano senza restrizione di tempo e di spazio".

L'area espositiva fu ripartita tra aree con strutture ed edifici permanenti, che avrebbero in seguito fatto parte del nuovo quartiere di Roma, ed aree, destinate solo all'Esposizione.

Secondo lo schema definitivo di raggruppamento delle mostre e iniziative per l'E42 varato nel gennaio 1941, l'Esposizione si sarebbe dovuta svolgere entro dieci sezioni minuziosamente definite. A grandi linee il progetto prevedeva un primo gruppo di padiglioni dedicati alla parte internazionale curata direttamente dai Paesi aderenti all'iniziativa.

---

[41] Cfr. G. L. Maffei, *Città di fondazione romana: lettura di impianti urbani pianificati*, Firenze 2002.

A questi seguivano le sezioni dedicate alle diverse città, tra le varie mostre un ruolo di primo piano assumeva la *Mostra della Civiltà italiana* che avrebbe dovuto esaltare il genio italiano quale si era espresso attraverso i secoli, dalle origini al regime fascista. Uno spazio espositivo piuttosto vasto era dedicato al P.N.F. ed alla *Città italiana dell'economia corporativa*, costituita dai quartieri del commercio, industria, artigianato, agricoltura, cooperazione e credito. Infine, il piano determinava gli spazi dedicati agli spettacoli e divertimenti con la realizzazione del *Teatro Imperiale* e della sezione cinema, quelli preposti ai vari servizi e in fine, come già accennato, l'area dei nuovi scavi di Ostia antica di cui si prevedeva il raddoppio della zona archeologica.

Come già accennato l'Esposizione del 1942 avrebbe dovuto creare le condizioni necessarie per consentire l'orientamento urbanistico di Roma verso il mare. La zona prescelta, quella delle Tre fontane, non rientrava nel piano regolatore generale dell'epoca né nella normativa governatoriale relativa ai cosiddetti nuclei edilizi. Per questo motivo si ricorse ad una legislazione speciale con la quale si procedette alla dichiarazione di pubblica utilità delle opere necessarie per l'Esposizione universale ed internazionale di Roma e per l'espansione di Roma verso il mare[42].

In sostanza le disposizioni di legge prevedevano che l'E42 fosse articolata da un recinto dell'Esposizione destinato alle opere necessarie alla realizzazione delle città per le mostre temporanee e permanenti; una zona

---

[42] Cfr. L. Di Majo, *L'E42 e l'autocelebrazione del regime*, in *Il parlamento italiano. Storia e politica dell'Italia 1861-1988*, vol. XII, tomo II, 1939-1945. *Dal «consenso» al crollo: dalla II guerra mondiale alla liberazione*, Milano 1990, pp. 54-58.

di ampliamento edilizio d'immediato contatto con l'E42 e una zona di espansione della città verso il mare[43].

L'adozione di successivi piani particolareggiati, che avrebbe dovuto seguire le espropriazioni del 1937, doveva consentire l'urbanizzazione di tali zone. In realtà il primo piano particolareggiato risale proprio al 1942, quando ormai l'idea dell'Esposizione era stata abbandonata a favore della costruzione del quartiere residenziale dell'EUR.

Lo scoppio della seconda guerra mondiale e l'entrata in guerra dell'Italia nel giugno del 1940 interruppero i lavori lasciando l'opera incompleta[44].

Destino imperiale

Più fortuna ebbe nella fase realizzativa, il progetto *Triennale d'Oltremare di Napoli*.

La proclamazione dell'Impero nel 1936 dopo la conquista dell'Etiopia proprio all'indomani della richiesta dell'E41-42, rendeva evidente, come il

---

[43] Cfr. *l'E42 in Roma: stato dei lavori e nuovi progetti. Le sistemazioni urbanistiche connesse: via Imperiale e nuova stazione di Roma Termini*, in «Architettura», fascicolo speciale, Milano, dicembre 1939.

[44] Dell'E42 restano oggi pochi "frammenti", l'intera documentazione progettuale prodotta, anche a livello di eseguibilità può essere considerata come una testimonianza unica sull'interpretazione dell'architettura come arte di Stato. Per un approfondimento sugli sviluppi dell'intero progetto *E42* cfr. *L'Esposizione Universale di Roma 1942*, in «Architettura», fascicolo speciale, Milano, dicembre 1938; L. Benevolo, *Storia dell'architettura moderna*, Bari 1981, pp. 623-625; R. Mariani, *E 42 : un progetto per l'ordine* nuovo, Milano 1987; T. Gregory, A. Tartaro, (a cura di), *E42. Utopia e scenario del regime*, vol. I, *Ideologia e propaganda per l'olimpiade della civiltà*, Venezia 1992; Ente Autonomo Esposizione Universale di Roma, (a cura di), *Leggi, decreti e provvedimenti: 1936-1996*, Roma 1996; R. Mariani, *Il luogo e il piano dell'E42*, in C. F. Carli, G. Mercurio, L. Prisco, *E42 – EUR. Segno e sogno del Novecento*, cit., pp. 26-27; C. Bertilaccio, F. Innamorati, *Eur SpA e il patrimonio di E42*, Roma 2005.

programma di confronto pacifico previsto dall'Esposizione romana fosse drammaticamente contraddetto da orizzonti di guerra che si andavano profilando fino al definitivo scoppio del secondo conflitto mondiale.

La conquista delle terre africane aveva consentito all'Italia di riconquistare, almeno idealmente, quel ruolo di nazione-guida di un impero coloniale e, dunque, di rivivere i fasti e la gloria che aveva già conosciuto in età romana.

Espansione, grandezza, impero, dunque, ma fortemente caratterizzati in senso italiano: il che comportava da un lato la pretesa negazione delle esperienze "straniere", dall'altro il recupero di alcuni dati di fatto peculiari del nostro paese[45].

In questo nuovo contesto imperiale, Napoli per la sua posizione strategica nel Mediterraneo, finì con l'assumere il ruolo fondamentale di testa di ponte dell'Impero e centro culturale ed economico-amministrativo dei rapporti con le colonie d'Africa per cui: "*...L'idea di una Mostra delle Terre Italiane d'Oltremare sembrò perfettamente normale ai più, negli anni immediatamente successivi a quelli della conquista cruenta dei territori dell'Africa Orientale...Si voleva attraverso una grandiosa Mostra, documentare la storia della conquista militare, riallacciandola alla campagna di Abissinia del 1896, così disastrosamente conclusasi, ed alle più recenti azioni militari in Tripolitania del 1911, glorificando il tempo ed il*

[45] C'è la tradizione linguistica e culturale che si estende oltre i confini dell'Italia, l'emigrazione, le colonie con milioni di italiani sparse in tutto il mondo. Ci sono gli ambienti economici milanesi inevitabilmente scettici di fronte al nazionalismo tipicamente «romano», intellettuale e letterario, ma sensibili ai temi della pace sociale, dell'interclassismo, dell'esaltazione del "fatto" produttivo, e di una realistica espansione economica e commerciale, cfr. G. Rumi, *L'imperialismo fascista*, Milano 1974, pp. 26-30.

regime fascista di fronte alla popolazione, ed illustrando infine l'opera di civilizzazione svolta nei nuovi territori, le possibilità di reperimento di nuove materie prime e soprattutto le qualità del nuovo "spazio vitale"..."[46].

D'altra parte, come è dettagliatamente specificato nel catalogo-documentario della *Triennale d'Oltremare*[47], Napoli ed il suo porto erano stati punti di partenza sia di truppe che di materiale bellico alla volta dell'Africa ed avevano diligentemente assolto il compito di centro di raccolta di tutto quanto doveva essere inviato in Africa[48]; sembrava ovvio prospettare la possibilità che Napoli divenisse un gran centro commerciale dei prodotti provenienti dall'Africa e "*...Per quanto in verità non si sapesse proprio bene quali prodotti si sarebbero potuti commerciare era tuttavia la diffusa opinione dei più quella di credere che qualche cosa si sarebbe fatto di queste terre d'Oltremare e che la nostra città dovesse trarne vantaggio anche in rapporto alla sua posizione geografica...*"[49].

---

[46] C. Cocchia, *L'Edilizia a Napoli dal 1918 al 1958*, Napoli 1961, p. 39.

[47] *"Il Duce, nelle ore fatidiche della Marcia su Roma, sicuro delle mete da raggiungere, ha assegnato a Napoli, con parole che ora appaiono mirabile profezia, il compito di porto dell'Impero; ed il porto di Napoli, dai sonanti suoi moli, dalle sue fervorose officine, dalle calate pulsanti di mille attività commerciali, dagli affollati cantieri, con le sue operose maestranze, leva osanna all'Uomo cui Idiio commise i destini e le fortune della Patria e rivolge con orgoglio lo sguardo alle mete raggiunte e documentate nella prima edizione della Mostra delle Terre d'Oltremare, mentre tende con ansia alle imminenti conquiste che consacreranno il suo destino di porto mediterraneo ed Imperiale..."*. Cfr. *Napoli porto dell'impero*, in *Prima Mostra Triennale delle Terre Italiane d'Oltremare...*, cit., p. 101.

[48] Sulla storia del porto di Napoli cfr. A. Assante, *Funzione mediterranea del porto di Napoli*, Napoli 1941; G. Menna, *Il porto di Napoli dall'Unità d'Italia alla Seconda Guerra Mondiale*, in B. Gravagnuolo, (a cura di), *Napoli, il porto e la città. Storia e progetti*, Napoli 1994, pp. 143-152; O. Ghiringhelli, *Napoli "Regina del Mediterraneo"*, in C. De Seta, (a cura di), *L'Architettura a Napoli tra le due guerre*, cit., pp. 135-142; F. De Sanctis, *Napoli un golfo per l'Europa*, Napoli 2002.

[49] C. Cocchia, *L'Edilizia a Napoli...*, cit. p. 40.

Napoli città con il destino di porto del Mediterraneo, già toccato a Marsiglia, città "coloniale" della Francia, con le Esposizioni coloniali del 1906 e del 1922[50] si appresta a costruire la nuova immagine dell'Italia imperiale.

I tempi di realizzazione dovranno essere brevissimi.

A Roma, nella sala del Mappamondo di palazzo Venezia, il 4 giugno 1938, Mussolini riceve il deputato Vincenzo Tecchio, Commissario Governativo della Mostra Triennale delle Terre Italiane d'Oltremare, il quale gli sottopone i programmi di dettaglio e i progetti tecnici ed architettonici della Mostra, in quella sede il duce dispone che gli Enti pubblici e privati interessati e soprattutto i Governi dell'Africa Orientale Italiana, della Libia e dell'Egeo, siano impegnati al successo della Triennale d'Oltremare, fissando l'inaugurazione per il 9 maggio 1940, XVIII dell'éra fascista[51].

Nonostante quest'ultima sia destinata ad essere assorbita dall'E42, come città effimera delle colonie, si presenta, nella sua veste definitiva, con un insieme urbanistico, architettonico ed artistico capace di trasmettere significati originali ed in parte autonomi.

Documenti, monumenti

Le due Mostre, solo nel progetto iniziale presentano il comune, duplice, obiettivo dello svolgimento di manifestazioni espositive e della

---

[50] Come per Marsiglia, di Napoli veniva enfatizzata la proiezione verso il sud del Mediterraneo. Cfr. C. Hodeir, M. Pierre, *L'Exposition coloniale*, Paris 1991.

[51] Cfr. *Per la Triennale d'Oltremare*, in E. e D. Susmel (a cura di), *Opera omnia di Benito Mussolini*, vol. XXIX, Firenze 1959, p. 112.

riorganizzazione urbana a carattere metropolitano[52]: per l'E42, la creazione di un nuovo quartiere e della rete di infrastrutture per la pianificazione ed il controllo dell'espansione urbana verso il mare, per la Triennale d'Oltremare nella volontà del regime di dar luogo ad un attrattore economico che fungesse da impulso al quartiere operaio che si andava realizzando al di là della collina di Posillipo (Fuorigrotta), in funzione anche del grande stabilimento metallurgico di Bagnoli (ILVA).

A Napoli si lavora per realizzare una grande macchina illustrativa senza trascurare la visione urbanistica ed architettonica d'insieme: nella nuova città dell'impero il modello cardodecumanico dell'E42 che guida lo schema compositivo nel sistema di ingresso viene come sfumato nell'articolazione complessa degli altri padiglioni. La singolarità del disegno del verde, che crea quasi sempre un rapporto di continuità tra le insule adiacenti, unitamente ai percorsi volutamente interrotti e sfalsati, contribuisce a rendere particolarmente complessa la matrice iniziale, funzionale e al tempo stesso suggestiva[53].

La concretezza espositiva fu ottenuta, soprattutto grazie alla capacità dei progettisti di creare un clima coloniale reso palpabile dalle ricostruzioni ambientali e dal carattere evocativo delle architetture e degli spazi fruibili

---

[52] La Triennale d'Oltremare si riferisce al modello dell'E42 esclusivamente per superare gli inconvenienti registrati nell'Esposizione di Parigi del 1937; quelli cioè derivanti dalla scelta di un'area troppo centrale: inconvenienti di traffico, di spazio, di costi, visto che molte opere provvisorie si sarebbero dovute distruggere alla fine della manifestazione.

[53] Il rigoroso Piano cardodecumanico progettato da Piacentini per l'E42, sembra qui attenuarsi nell'articolazione dei padiglioni e degli spazi verdi. Sugli sviluppi del Piano Regolatore dell'E42 cfr. A. Muntoni, *Via dell'Impero tra "Forma Urbis" e piano della grande Roma*, in «Parametro», n. 138, Bologna-Faenza 1985, pp. 31-42.

che si pone, in certo modo, in continuità con la visionarietà delle Esposizioni Universali ed Internazionali dell'800.

Nella fase attuativa il Piano della città delle colonie di Napoli venne segnato da una profonda dicotomia tra due tipi diversi di culture facenti riferimento la prima al razionalismo, la seconda all'eclettismo e al monumentalismo classicista, dovendo far coesistere esigenze di carattere pratico ad esigenze propagandistiche.

Nella Mostra di Napoli si concretizza un progetto di città-parco, nella quale il verde è concepito esclusivamente come pubblico e dove l'insieme configura una completa integrazione tra complessi architettonici emergenti e componente naturalistica di fondo[54].

Viceversa a Roma si progetta una Esposizione Universale su un territorio sconfinato (oltre quatto milioni di mq), di cui solo un sesto è destinato ai padiglioni mentre il rimanente doveva costituire un sistema di parchi, giardini, piazze e strade[55]. È evidente che il regime voleva costruire un quartiere urbano nel quale inserire un'Esposizione Universale.

Lavorando nel senso contrario a tutte le altre Esposizioni Universali precedenti - Bruxelles, Parigi, Barcellona, New York – dove furono utilizzati tutti gli elementi dell'Esposizione stessa, per organizzare poi dei nuovi

---

[54] Cfr. C. Cocchia, *Architettura del verde e fontane alla Triennale d'Oltremare*, Napoli 1940. Nel saggio Cocchia chiarisce quali sono i principi ispiratori del complesso espositivo partenopeo: il verde e l'acqua, nell'equilibrio architettonico generale, hanno composto con gli spazi e con gli edifici un unico "quadro" dalle molteplici prospettive.

[55] *"...In quanto città, l'Esposizione non potrà nascere che con un impianto rigorosamente regolare; e vedremo infatti come il rigido e simmetrico reticolo della «città» futura del marzo del 1037 avrà completamente il sopravvento su ogni divagazione naturalistica..."*, E. Guidoni, *L'E 42, città della rappresentazione...*, cit., p. 30.

quartieri urbani, a Roma si è passati in primo luogo alla progettazione e costruzione di un nuovo quartiere urbano[56].

L'E42 fu impostata fin dall'inizio come un'esposizione senza precedenti né analogie con quelle realizzate fino allora. Avrebbe dovuto essere utopia costruita: i suoi palazzi, le sue piazze pensate come antichi fori, il suo stesso stile lontano dal tempo storico del classicismo come dal modernismo, fondato sulla categoria dell'assenza, dell'astrazione, del silenzio e dell'astrazione, furono considerati elementi indispensabili per la costruzione della città ideale.

Nella Triennale d'Oltremare questa visione sembra attenuarsi, poiché gran parte degli edifici fu costruita con carattere semi-permanente; non cambia però l'idea cioè quella di realizzare un città ideale[57], seppur effimera[58].

L'incompiuta E42 rappresentò la prima ed unica rifondazione della città di Roma, al di fuori dello stratificato tessuto storico, con un progetto di nucleo urbano separato, un centro satellite collegato a Roma da una grande arteria di comunicazione quale doveva essere la Via Imperiale, mentre la Mostra d'Oltremare riallacciandosi alla tradizione delle grandi esposizioni all'atto dell'inaugurazione si è presentata come un parco urbano attrezzato, la sua vocazione espositiva è stata alterata, nel corso degl'anni, dalla *damnatio memorie* post-bellica che ne ha condizionato e condiziona la sopravvivenza.

---

[56] R. Aloi, *Esposizioni. Architetture e Allestimenti*, Milano 1960.

[57] S. Samek Lodovici, *La fabbrica della città ideale*, in «Le Vie d'Italia», a. XLIV, n. 11, novembre 1938, 1351-1360.

[58] Cfr. D. Orlacchio, *La Città Ideale. Architettura e Architetti del Ventennio*, in «I Quaderni de Il Cerchio», n. 2, *La Ricerca dello Stato nuovo*, Napoli 1996, pp. 63-74.

La Triennale d'Oltremare doveva costituire l'attrattore socio-economico di un quartiere operaio di edilizia popolare e di ciò oggi ne conserva le caratteristiche; come l'attitudine ad una multifunzionalità, sempre nell'ambito di attività espositive, congressuali, culturali, ludiche e sportive[59].

L'E42-EUR, invece, non completato nell'obiettivo originario dell'Esposizione Universale, ha perseguito la soluzione "elitaria" nella realizzazione di un quartiere destinato ad una categoria sociale medio-alta; caratterizzato peraltro, dalla presenza di uffici, attività professionali, attratte dalla funzione direzionale che va assumendo sempre più il quartiere[60].

La Mostra d'Oltremare vive all'interno del suo contesto urbanistico, con il "filtro" della sua cinta muraria che non lo ha però preservato da danni sopraffazioni e superfetazioni; mentre l'EUR ha decisamente mutato l'approccio territoriale, soprattutto nel dopoguerra, e le modalità espositive, assumendo nuove finalità istituzionali con la costruzione di un vero e proprio quartiere urbano[61].

---

[59] Cfr. D. Orlacchio, *Il dibattito urbanistico e il Piano del '39*, in «I Quaderni de Il Cerchio», n. 2, *La Ricerca dello Stato Nuovo. Napoli: Urbanistica e Architettura del Ventennio*, Napoli 1997, pp. 81-102.

[60] Funzione direzionale che a Napoli era stata garantita, invece, dalla realizzazione ad opera del regime della *city* nella centrale zona del Rione Carità. Per un approfondimento sulle trasformazioni del Rione Carità durante il ventennio fascista cfr. P. Cislaghi, *La città fascista. Il rione Carità e la Mostra triennale delle Terre Italiane d'Oltremare*, cit., pp. 115-120.

[61] Attualmente l'Eur oltre che zona residenziale, è sede di uffici, sia pubblici che privati, tra cui la Confindustria, il Ministero della Salute, il Ministero delle Comunicazioni, la sede centrale dell'Eni,la sede centrale della Banca di Roma, nonché le sedi italiane di numerose multinazionali. A testimoniare l'originaria vocazione espositiva del quartiere, destinata a trasformarsi in un articolato complesso museale, restano, tra gli altri, il Museo della Civiltà Romana, il Museo Nazionale Preistorico Etnografico Luigi Pigorini, la sede dell'Archivio

Appendice

Centrale di Stato, un planetario con annesso Museo dell'Astronomia, inaugurato nel 2004, cfr. P. Scaglione, *Eur a Roma. Controguida d'architettura*, Torino 2000.

MOSTRA TRIENNALE DELLE TERRE ITALIANE D'OLTREMARE

D U C E

Nell'eseguire il Vostro ambitissimo ordine di organizzare la Mostra Triennale delle Terre Italiane d'Oltremare, Napoli intende raggiungere tre scopi:

1) Fare plasticamente il punto della risorta potenza imperiale italiana.
2) Dare prova delle sue capacità organizzative.
3) Mostrarsi degna della Vostra benevolenza e delle funzioni alle quali è chiamata dalla romana storia mediterranea di cui Voi siete l'Artefice.

Nel tendere a questi scopi, essa si sente più che mai romana e fascista. Napoli che a
Vostri Legionari ha dato l'ultimo e caloroso viatico della Patria, ha ricordato e ricorda, con commosso orgoglio, che Pozzuoli fu il primo grande Porto Mediterraneo di Roma, che con le opere militari e navali di Cuma e dei laghi di Lucrino e di Averno, Ottaviano costituì la prima salda base difensiva ed offensiva per consolidare il suo potere, che lo stesso Ottaviano, ormai Augusto, fece di Misero la base della più potente ed agguerrita flotta romana, che le grandi ombre di Scipione l'Africano e dei suoi Legionari giganteggiano ancora in quella Liternum che i romani fondarono ed il Fascismo risanò dalla palude e dalla malaria.

In questo mussoliniano rinnovarsi di fortune imperiali, Napoli sa quale sia la sua posizione geografica e storica, e ne avverte tutta la responsabilità.

La responsabilità cioè di dover diventare città complementare di Roma, Complementare di Roma in pace ed in guerra: testa di ponte per pacifici traffici marittimi ed aerei e base difensiva e offensiva navale ed aerea dell'Impero: accogliente, riposante, ospitale per gli amici che vengono alla città eterna e a Voi, decisamente ostile verso i nemici.

E così Napoli, che fu la più costante nella fedeltà alla Roma dei Cesari, rinsalda, dopo secoli, con la Roma di Mussolini la sua fraternità.

È un segno del destino, forse, che il Silurificio italiano scelga per sua più grande sede il seno di Baia, quando a pochi passi le ricerche archeologiche offrono la impressionante visione della Piscina Mirabilis, che fu il grande serbatoio idrico della flotta misenate; che Ansaldo ed Ilva potenzino la loro attrezzatura mentre si cerca di riaprire al traffico la gloriosa galleria militare di Cocceo che fece di Cuma, Averno e Misero un formidabile triangolo di guerra.

Ecco, perché, Duce, fra le tante ragioni che ci hanno convinti di scegliere la Zona Flegrea per sede della Mostra delle Terre Italiane d'Oltremare, una più di tutte è stata decisiva: quella di avvicinare Napoli a Roma, di porre l'avvenire della nostra città sulla via Appia, che fu la più romana fra le vie di Roma.

Napoli, 20 ottobre 1937/XV

V. Tecchio

ASNA, GP, Secondo Versamento, f. 879, *Lettera del presidente dell'Ente Autonomo Mostra Triennale d'Oltremare V. Tecchio a B. Mussolini.*

PER LA MOSTRA DELLE TERRE D'OLTREMARE

NAPOLI

Relazione dell'Architetto ALBERTO CALZA BINI

R. PREFETTURA, 21 DICEMBRE 1938 (relazione inviata a sua Eccellenza il PREFETTO di Napoli)

Eccellenza,

A seguito della lettera in data 27-10-1936-XIV con la quale l'Eccellenza Vostra mi dava incarico di procedere allo studio per la scelta dell'area più indicata per la futura Esposizione delle "Terre d'oltremare", che avrà luogo in Napoli ogni tre anni con carattere permanente, ho esaminato le località che, a mio giudizio, potevano sembrare più adatte per estensione ubicazione e possibilità d'accesso.
La zona di Capodichino, pianeggiante ed ampia, resulta ormai acquisita all'aereoporto militare; e d'altra parte sarebbe stata meno indicata per il carattere dei quartieri di attraversamento per l'accesso.
Le vaste aree libere nei pressi del nuovo grande ospedale che visitai anche col Podestà Avv. Orgera, si rivelarono anche poco adatte per la natura assai movimentata del terreno e per la lontananza, assoluta e relativa, dal centro di Napoli.
Altre località di possibile utilizzazione rimanevano: il Parco della Rimembranza a Posillipo e la vastissima zona dei Campi Flegrei fuori Grotta.
A favore del Parco della Rimembranza militerebbe senza dubbio la bellezza incomparabile del panorama che da ogni parte si apre tutt'intorno alla paradisiaca collina; l'esistenza di strade intorno al Parco, la convenienza di utilizzare una zona già collegata con Napoli e pochissimo frequentata anche per pubbliche passeggiate.
A contrapposto di tali vantaggi devono però elencarsi:

1. La impossibilità di procedere a costruzioni di carattere permanente in una zona naturalmente panoramica e assai opportunamente destinata a parco;
2. la scarsità di vie di accesso specialmente durante i lavori di preparazione della Mostra per i materiali, carriaggi, ecc.;
3. la insufficienza di spazio: meno di 100.000 mq. di area, anche sacrificando una grandissima parte del terreno destinato a parco o a zona di rispetto panoramico.

La pianura dei Campi Flegrei presenta invece, su tutte le altre, grande disponibilità di area libera pianeggiante, servita da numerose vie di comunicazione. La principale di queste è certo la galleria di Posillipo, la quale però nelle condizioni attuali può dirsi essere stata, più che mezzo di comunicazione principale, causa della separazione tra il quartiere fuori Grotta e la città vera e propria.

Tale inconveniente dovuto alle instabili condizioni della galleria, alla impalcatura che ne ostruisce parte del transito, alla mancanza di rivestimento e di illuminazione, dovrebbe essere senz'altro rimosso prima di ogni inizio di relazioni della Mostra.

La cosa non appare difficile quando si pensi all'enorme vantaggio che la rapidità e la facilità della comunicazione tra il quartiere di Mergellina e il quartiere di Fuori Grotta darà alla città di Napoli, la quale verrà veramente ad assicurarsi una vasta zona di espansione in località piana vicina e ottimamente servita da altri sussidiari mezzi di comunicazione.

E sono proprio tali mezzi sussidiari: la comunicazione che dal Vomero o dal quartiere di via Manzoni per la scesa della Canzanella porta al viale di Agnano; la nuova via di attraversamento della collina di Posillipo; la ferrovia Cumana; e, soprattutto, la direttissima per Roma e il suo servizio metropolitano, che si può dire designino la zona dei Campi Flegrei come la naturalmente adatta al sorgere di una grande Mostra.

Infatti non soltanto la ferrovia metropolitana con il grande edificio per stazione viaggiatori che sorge sulla piazza di Campi Flegrei potrà ottimamente servire per l'afflusso dei viaggiatori a Mostra aperta, ma, durante il periodo di preparazione e di febbrile lavoro, il collegamento ferroviario nella zona stessa permetterà rapidità ed economia per tutti i trasporti.

A completare l'elenco delle vie di comunicazione e di accesso è opportuno tener presente la convenienza di riaprire anche la primitiva galleria presso Mergellina, la quale dovrebbe essere modernamente attrezzata a doppio piano per il percorso tramviario e per quello automobilistico.
Resta ancora a considerare il secondo degli inconvenienti che sono causa del mancato sviluppo del quartiere di Fuori Grotta; e cioè la condizione veramente deplorevole e fatiscente e di mancanza di pulizia in cui si trova tutto il vecchio quartiere che può dirsi abbandonato a sé stesso e per il quale è da invocare il piccone risanatore per il decoro di Napoli e per il regolare espandersi della Città.
La opportuna e tempestiva demolizione anche di una sola parte del quartiere detto il Castellano, potrà permettere l'apertura di una larga e moderna via di accesso che dall'imbocco della galleria dovrebbe rapidamente raggiungere la parte più moderna e sana del quartiere presso la piazza dei Campi Flegrei.
Ho voluto far presenti subito gli inconvenienti e le opportunità e possibilità della loro rimozione, perché sono convinto che la necessità di provvedere ad attrezzare la Città per ospitare la grande Mostra che il Duce ha voluto assegnare a Napoli riconoscendola degna sede di una consacrazione delle nostre aspirazioni e delle nostre attività nelle Terre d'oltremare, deve risolversi in una immediata opera urbanistica di risanamento e di ampliamento della stessa Città; e sono altrettanto convinto che la organizzazione della Mostra in funzione anche di quest'opera di risanamento e di espansione raggiungerà benefici scopi nell'interesse di Napoli. E' doveroso aggiungere che già la Commissione sindacale che ha studiato e predisposto il nuovo Piano Regolatore della Città aveva previsto, pur senza lontanamente prevedere una così prossima e grandiosa realizzazione, la possibilità di riservare una parte della zona di Fuori Grotta proprio alle mostre periodiche di Napoli che per la sua importanza e per il suo destino non avrebbe dovuto a lungo esserne priva.
La zona complessivamente libera nelle condizioni attuali comprende circa due milioni di mq.- Ma anche lasciando considerevole parte disponibile per il nuovo sfruttamento edilizio, può ritenersi più che sufficiente una riserva di un milione di mq., di cui più della metà potrebbero essere utilizzati e coperti per la I° Mostra del 1938-39.
Tale estensione è in parte di proprietà della Società Edilizia Laziale alla quale dovrebbe essere espropriata, salvo opportuna transazione

considerato che la detta Società potrà beneficiare della messa in valore della zona per quella parte di area di cui resterà proprietaria.
Per l'esproprio della restante area sarà opportuno procedere alla dichiarazione di pubblica utilità della esecuzione della Mostra.
Allego una planimetria nella quale sono segnate le due zone di Posillipo e di Fuori Grotta, con la indicazione delle vie di accesso. A conclusione ritengo che la scelta dell'area sia di facile definizione, e che la zona dei Campi Flegrei o Fuori Grotta sia senz'altro da preferire.

Con distinta osservanza
Arch. Alberto Calza Bini

ASNA, GP, Secondo Versamento, f. 879; *Per la Mostra delle Terre d'Oltremare. Relazione di Alberto Calza Bini.*

AGENZIA STEFANI

ANNO LXXXVII ROMA 27 SETTEMBRE 1939 ANNO XVII, N. 3, Ore 13.02

Napoli, il recente ordine del Duce, di continuare i lavori della Mostra della Triennale delle Terre Italiane d'Oltremare con la necessaria tempestività perché la Mostra venga regolarmente inaugurata il giorno fissato dal calendario del regime, e cioè il 9 maggio 1940-XVIII, richiama l'attenzione su questa grande e documentata rassegna che sarà una vera e propria sagra dell'espansione italiana nei secoli.

Su un totale previsto di circa 900.000 mc. di costruzioni, disposti in 54 edifici, già 640.000 mc. sono stati ultimati, con 1.100.000 mc di movimenti di terra, 223.000 mq di superfici stradali sono stati coperti e l'area destinata a parchi, giardini, cortili – di ben 290.000 mq. – è anche essa completamente sistemata. Come sistemati già sono i servizi della Mostra: 12 km. di acquedotto e 12 km di fognature. 15 km. di rete elettrica ad alta tensione e i 17 km. a bassa tensione sono in allestimento.
Anche l'attrezzatura della flora si manifesta già imponente: su una superficie alberata di 210.000 mq. sono state messe a dimora 14.000 piante d'alto fusto, delle quali oltre 2.000 sono state appositamente trasportate dall'Africa Italiana. Oltre 265.000 piante sono state acclimatate in appositi vivai e serviranno a formare aiuole, siepi, festoni decorativi.
Duemilacinquecento operai – che hanno già all'attivo 800.000 giornate lavorative – lavorano assiduamente alle fabbriche, ai parchi e alle strade della Mostra mentre sono in costruzione la Casa del Fascio e la funivia che su un percorso di 1.600 m. allaccerà la Mostra a Posillipo alto.
Sono stati già banditi 18 concorsi, a carattere artistico, architettonico, etnografico, fotografico e altri concorsi ancora sono in elaborazione, sono stati anche preordinati 25 congressi a carattere nazionale. Inoltre sono in preparazione due Mostre d'arte, una mostra filatelica, una numismatica e una fotografica, varie esposizioni merceologiche e tutto un complesso di spettacoli e di manifestazioni teatrali, musicali, artistiche, culturali, scientifiche, sportive che serviranno a rendere viva e fervida, nei suoi settori, questa rassegna dell'espansione e della potenza italica nei secoli. (Stefani)

ACS, PCM, 14.1.91, anni 1937-1939, busta n. 2483.

MOSTRA TRIENNALE DELLE TERRE ITALIANE D'OLTREMARE

CONVEGNI, RADUNI E CONGRESSI CHE SI TERRANNO PRESSO LA TRIENNALE DAL 9 MAGGIO AL 15 OTTOBRE XVIII°:

1. Botanica, 12 – 13 maggio;
2. Convegno Scolastico Coloniale 14 – 15 – 16 maggio;
3. Diritto Commerciale e Industriale 17 – 18 – 19 maggio;
4. Pediatria 20 – 21 – 22 maggio;
5. Biologia sperimentale 24 – 25 – 26 maggio;
6. Materiali da costruzione 27 – 28 – 29 maggio;
7. Medicina Legale 30 – 31 maggio – 1° giugno;
8. Scrittori coloniali 20 – 30 giugno;
9. G.U.F. 19 – 20 luglio Convegno, 15 – 20 luglio Cine Guf, 15 – 20 luglio Teatro Guf, 15 – 21 luglio Raduno Guf;
10. Raduno dei chimici 25 – 30 luglio;
11. 1° Convegno delle Scuole Sindacali 30 – 31 agosto, 1 – 2 settembre;
12. Ispettori onorari 3 – 4 – 5 – 6 – 7 – 8 settembre;
13. Deputazioni Storia Patria 8 – 9 – 10 settembre;
14. Zoologia e Entomologia 11 – 12 – 13 –14 settembre;
15. Filatelico 14 – 15 – 16 settembre;
16. Malattie Tropicali 15 – 16 – 17 – 18 settembre;
17. Convegno sulla Colonizzazione 19 – 26 settembre;
18. Dirigenti Aziende Industriali 27 – 28 – 29 settembre;
19. Studi Coloniali 4 – 5 – 6 – 7 – 8 ottobre;
20. Antropologia e Etnologia 4 – 5 – 6 – 7 – 8 ottobre;
21. Dermatologia e Sifilografia 10 – 11 – 12 ottobre;
22. Paleontologia umana 16 – 17 – 18 ottobre;
23. Storia del Risorgimento...............ottobre;
24. I° Convegno Nazionale per lo sviluppo delle Relazioni Industriali con i Territori Italiani d'Oltremare;

25. Congresso del Sindacato Nazionale dei Medici: "I danni dell'iperalimentazione negli adulti";
26. Riunione Straordinaria del Consiglio Nazionale delle Accademie;
27. Congresso di Diritto Penale Coloniale;
28. Convegno Artiste e Laureate.

DI ALCUNI CONGRESSI NON E' STATA ANCORA FISSATA LA DATA; ALTRI 10

CIRCA SONO NELLA FASE ORGANIZZATIVA

ACS, PCM, 14.1.91, anni 1937-1939, busta n. 2483.

MOSTRA TRIENNALE DELLE TERRE ITALIANE D'OLTREMARE

Pubblicazioni edite a cura e a spesa della Mostra Triennale:

1 – Lidio Cipriani Le abitazioni indigene in A.O.I.
2 – Paolo Graziosi L'arte rupestre in Libia
3 – Giuseppe Scortecci L'ambiente biologico del Sahara
4 – Amedeo Maiuri La zona archeologica della Triennale
5- Molajoli – Ortolani – De Filippis: L'Oriente nell'arte Italiana
6 – Catalogo della Mostra d'Arte Contemporanea
7 – Catalogo della Mostra del P.N.F.
8 – Catalogo generale della Triennale
9 – Documentario della Triennale
10 – Atti di vari congressi.

PER TUTTE LE PUBBLICAZIONI SARÀ USATA LA CARTA FABBRICATA CON CELLULOSA DI ALFA E SPARTO LIBICI.

20 febbraio 1940.

ACS, PCM, 14.1.91, anni 1937-1939, busta n. 2483.

MOSTRA TRIENNALE DELLE TERRE ITALIANE D'OLTREMARE

OPERE D'ARTE DELLA TRIENNALE

Scultura – pittura - affreschi- ecc……………………………£ 1.641.000

Mosaici………………………………………………………………………£ 456.000

Totale……………………………………………………………………..£ 2.097.000

ACS, PCM, 14.1.91, anni 1937-1939, busta n. 2483.

Roma 11/7/1939-XVII

Consigliere Nazionale Tecchio

NAPOLI

A seguito delle conversazioni avute con te e con il collega Maiuri in merito alla cessione temporanea di una parte del materiale della Mostra Augustea della Romanità per la Triennale delle Terre d'Oltremare, sono ancora costretto a precisarti quanto ebbi occasione di dirti a vice; che cioè, avendo il Duce dichiarata permanente la Mostra Augustea, il materiale raccolto per essa si trova, soltanto per necessità contingenti, attualmente immagazzinato a causa del trasferimento della Mostra nel Palazzo delle Esposizioni di via nazionale al palazzo che verrà eretto nella zona dell'E.42, ma esso costituisce anche ora un'unità inscindibile, e, del resto rimarrà nella sua attuale collocazione ancora soltanto per pochi mesi in attesa della sua definitiva sistemazioni nel palazzo costruito appositamente nella zona dell'Esposizione Universale di Roma. Tale materiale è stato tutto acquistato con fondi concessi personalmente dal Duce; pertanto in merito alla vostra richiesta io dovrò riferire a chi di dovere prima di poter dare una definitiva risposta.

Desidererei però che mi venissero intanto fornite precise assicurazioni sui seguenti punti:

1) che tutto indistintamente il materiale che verrà ceduto temporaneamente alla Mostra Triennale delle Terre d'Oltremare ci verrà restituito per il settembre 1940 e in ogni caso non oltre la fine di quell'anno se la chiusura della predetta esposizione dovesse essere prorogata oltre la data attualmente prevista o anche se la Esposizione divenisse permanente.
2) che tutto il materiale sarà trasportato con le opportune cautele e sarà assicurato contro qualsiasi rischio in base alle stime che forniremo; dal momento in cui esce da nostri magazzini al momento in cui vi rientrerà.
3) che su ciascun pezzo inviato a Napoli verrà indicato esplicitamente che è esposto dalla Mostra della Romanità.
4) che in cambio dell'autorizzazione concessa e in compenso del prestito di tali oggetti, il materiale che verrà preparato ex-novo per la Sezione Romana a cura della Triennale delle Terre d'Oltremare sarà tutto o in parte ceduto alla Mostra della Romanità ed eventualmente in quale misura.

Attendo in proposito un tuo cortese cenno di risposta.

f/to Giglioli

ACS, PCM, 14.1.91, anni 1937-1939, busta n. 2483.

settembre 1939 anno XVII

Presidenze del Consiglio dei Ministri

Gabinetto

APPUNTO PER IL DUCE

Il prof.Giglioli ha fatto presente che il programma definitivo della Mostra Triennale delle Terre Italiane d'Oltremare comprenderà apposita sezione riservata a "Roma antica sul Mare", alla cui realizzazione attende l'Accademico Maiuri.

Per l'allestimento di tale padiglione il commissario governativo della Mostra d'Oltremare ha chiesto in prestito il seguente materiale, già esposto alla Mostra Augustea:

-Plastici N.18

-Fotografie, piante e disegni N.26

-Riproduzioni galvaniche e piccoli calchi N.4

-Calchi di statue, ritratti, rilievi ed epigrafi N.47

In via di massima sono già state studiate le modalità secondo le quali tale prestito potrebbe aver luogo ed il Consigliere Tecchio ha date le più ampie rassicurazioni per la conservazione del materiale, promettendo formalmente che sarebbe restituito entro il 1940-XVIII, anche se la Mostra fosse prorogata o trasformata in permanente.

Prima di concretare le opportune intese, il prof. Giglioli ha chiesto l'autorizzazione di questa Presidenza, esprimendo al riguardo parere favorevole.

Per le determinazioni del Duce.

ACS, PCM, 14.1.91, anni 1937-1939, busta n. 2483.

SIGNIFICATO DELLA MOSTRA TRIENNALE DELLE TERRE D'OLTREMARE

Quando, nel maggio 1940, si inaugurò a Napoli la Prima Mostra Triennale delle Terre d'Oltremare, la guerra già incombeva inesorabile ai nostri confini. Ed ora, dopo tante amarezze, tante disillusioni, tanti lutti e rovine, potrebbe anche apparire frutto di inconsulta imprevidenza aver impegnato una somma così ingente di energie e di capitali in un momento non certo favorevole ad iniziative del genere. E realmente dalla guerra la Mostra ebbe troncata la vita e i suoi fecondi sviluppi. Eppure, appunto dal profondo contrasto con la gravità dell'ora essa acquistò un significato trascendente di gran lunga l'entità stessa del suo imponente complesso materiale; e più ancora lo acquista oggi e lo acquisterà domani, quali che siano le vicissitudini della grande bufera che travolge il mondo, in quanto ha segnato comunque un punto fermo a cui si deve e si dovrà far capo nella realistica considerazione del nostro divenire.

Con la Triennale si volle, allora, documentare in una completa sintesi panoramica l'opera compiuta dal genio, dal valore e dal lavoro italiano in terra di colonia: si vollero fissare le caratteristiche storiche, geografiche ed economiche dei nostri possedimenti; si vollero dedurre, dal comparato esame di questa opera e di queste caratteristiche, le direttrici fondamentali per la futura azione; si volle infine offrire al mondo, diffidente o ignaro, in buona e in mala fede, la possibilità di una valutazione obiettiva della nostra volontà e capacità costruttrici e civilizzatrici.

Ma si volle anche, e soprattutto, al di là di ogni contingente motivo politico, e indipendentemente da circostanze e scopi transeunti, dimostrare la continuità storica e ideale della nostra inesauribile forza di espansione.

E in questo senso effettivamente la Mostra, oltre che espressione del fervore coloniale e colonizzatore allora in atto, apparve quasi coronamento di tutto un ciclo di volontà, di sacrifici e di sforzi maturatisi non soltanto attraverso gli anni e i decenni più vicini, ma attraverso i secoli, i millenni anzi, dell'espansione oltremare delle nostre genti.

Per questo e da questo la giustificazione storica della grande manifestazione napoletana, diremmo quasi la sua inderogabilità, la sua sostanziale rispondenza al momento cruciale della situazione interna e internazionale. Un grande sforzo militare ed economico era stato testè compiuto per l'affermazione della nostra potenza coloniale: sforzo che assumeva ancor più ingente valore e significato, se posto in diretta connessione con tutto il precedente movimento avente per oggetto l'oltremare. Prima di procedere oltre sull'arduo cammino e soprattutto prima che la guerra ci trascinasse nel suo grande gorgo, era opportuno sostare un momento per raccogliere le fila dell'ingente lavoro compiuto, fissarle in una definita documentazione, ad un duplice essenziale scopo, anche se non palese: quello di trarne, con gli opportuni insegnamenti, nuova lena per gli sviluppi della intrapresa azione; e quello, nella deprecata ipotesi di una sosta più o meno lunga imposta dagli avvenimenti, di lasciare alle venienti generazioni il monito (fatto eloquente dall'evidenza di queste documentazioni) a non dimenticare il passato recente e lontano e a riprenderne appena possibile il corso, facendo tesoro della somma di esperienze acquisita in tanto lungo travaglio.

Lasciamo stare i capitali impegnati e non recuperati, il valore materiale e affettivo delle raccolte, delle costruzioni, di tutta la imponente organizzazione spettacolare – valore che la guerra può aver distrutto anche totalmente con ingente sacrificio e danno del lavoro compiuto e dello stesso nostro patrimonio artistico, civile ed economico da esso rappresentato – lasciamo stare tutto ciò che è legato all'attrezzatura contingente della manifestazione. L'importanza essenziale e funzionale della Mostra resta e resterà intatta, i suoi risultati intenzionali hanno acquistato e acquisteranno anzi maggiore evidenza dalla drammatica involuzione degli avvenimenti.

Un popolo che, in tutte le fasi della sua antichissima storia, ha dato tante prove della sua vitalità, non può morire, anche se la tempesta sembra sommergerlo. Tante volte è stato travolto da tempeste foss'anche più terribili e disastrose. Eppure sempre ha riassommato, dopo periodi più o meno lunghi di crisi: segno dell'intima vitalità della stirpe. E questa vitalità ha dimostrato appunto irradiandosi sulle vie del mondo, sotto le multiformi vesti dell'uomo di mare e del mercante, dell'avventuriero e del missionario, dell'esploratore e dello scienziato, del lavoratore manuale e dell'artista, dell'emigrante e del soldato, a seconda delle circostanze e delle personali attitudini. Espansione individuale o collettiva, sporadica od organizzata, ma comunque tale da far considerare essenziale l'apporto costruttivo delle nostre genti al grande movimento colonizzatore che, pur nell'alterna vicenda di ombre e di luci, è superiore espressione della marcia

della civiltà in tutto il mondo per la conquista di un più alto livello di vita morale e materiale, senza discriminazioni di razze e di ambienti.
Se un tale apporto si è manifestato in epoche e condizioni tanto differenti, ciò significa che la proclamata forza espansiva e la virtù colonizzatrice del nostro paese non son vuote affermazioni rettoriche di esaltazione nazionalistica, né frutto di audaci piani di imperialismo politico ed economico, bensì una realtà che affonda le sue radici in un effettivo complesso di fattori ed esigenze legato a fondamentali peculiarità del nostro spirito e del nostro territorio. La stessa tradizione millenaria e la somma di esperienze accumulate di generazione in generazione costituiscono poi un ulteriore e non ultimo incentivo al persistente rinverdirsi di questa fondamentale linea direttrice della esistenza nazionale, per cui l'oltremare è per noi condizione insopprimibile di vita e di prosperità.
In considerazione di tutto ciò noi abbiamo ferma fede nelle capacità di ripresa della nostra Italia e sul suo dignitoso ritorno al posto che le compete in una pacifica convivenza delle Nazioni su basi di equità internazionale. Il lavoro e l'intelligenza italiani ritorneranno ad essere strumento di civiltà sulle vie del mondo.
Un tanto grande passato non può distruggersi o dimenticarsi. In questo appunto sta il significato sostanziale e duraturo della Triennale di Napoli, anche se essa non dovesse riprendere la sua stabile continuità di organizzazione attiva e permanente. Nella quale ipotesi anzi vorremmo che essa non rimanesse un vago ricordo, ma potesse perpetuarsi proprio in questo suo aspetto essenziale con la accurata conservazione di tutto il

materiale che sia possibile recuperare e, parallelamente, con la pubblicazione, o per lo meno con l'approntamento per la pubblicazione dei tanti elementi raccolti.

Materiale ed elementi, questi, affluiti a Napoli attraverso una organizzazione capillare ed estesissima, affidata ai maggiori competenti dei singoli settori e i cui risultati, tra di loro coordinati in un quadro dalle proporzioni assolutamente insolite, sarebbe realmente una incommensurabile perdita se dovessero andar dispersi, appunto perché precisamente dalla loro coordinazione hanno derivato tanto straordinaria importanza.

A sottolineare la eccezionale ricchezza qualitativa e quantitativa del materiale raccolto dall'Ente ordinatore basterà ricordare la successione delle singole sezioni con gli argomenti trattati:

Roma antica sul mare: mito campano di Enea; conquista romana del Mediterraneo; le province romane d'oltremare (i porti d'Italia, tecnica costruttiva navale, province romane d'oltremare, Roma verso l'Oriente); marina mercantile; il trionfo romano; simbolo di Roma navale.

Repubbliche marinare: l'espansione delle Repubbliche (ripresa della navigazione, espansione di Pisa, espansione di Genova); sacrario delle reliquie; la quarta crociata; armeria (fondaco veneziano portico della navigazione); Genova dei secoli XV-XVI-XVII; espansione veneziana in Levante; il trono dogale; ordinamento civile di Venezia; diplomazia veneziana; battaglia di Lepanto; la guerra di Candia; gli ultimi anni della Repubblica di Venezia; marina ligure, sarda, toscana e pontificia; marina napoletana.

La Galea di Marco Querini

L'Oltremare e la pittura italiana dal sec. XV al sec. XVIII: arazzi fiorentini; Carpaccio, Bellini, Santacroce; Mansueti e Belliniano; Dossi, Tiziano, Bronzino; Tintoretto e Tiziano; i Secentisti; i Settecentisti; G.D. Tiepolo; Luca Giordano.

Pionieri ed esploratori italiani in Africa: cartografia dagli albori del medio Evo alla fine del secolo XVIII; 1800-1850; 1850-1875; 1875-1885; 1885-1897; 1897-1940; Duca degli Abruzzi.

Conquiste coloniali: l'Africa nel 1869; Eritrea; Somalia; Libia; 1869-1935; la conquista dell'Impero (episodio di Ual-Ual; lo sforzo delle armi italiane; le battaglie; la conquista; i trofei; armi del nemico.

Partito Nazionale Fascista: il giuramento; l'800 politico e coloniale; realtà coloniale mussoliniana; il volontarismo fascista; l'esperimento sanzionista; l'epopea legionaria in Africa; la guerra civile in Spagna; l'aiuto alla Spagna Nazionale; il Sacrario.

Lavoro italiano in Africa: Suez; Egitto e Sudan; Angola, Mozambico, Sud-Africa, Gibuti; Congo; Kenia, Tanganica, Tenerife; Algeria, Marocco, Senegal, Tangeri; Tunisia.

Espansione Italiana in Oriente: età romana; secolo XIII; torre di marco Polo; secolo XIV; secolo XV; secolo XVI; secolo XVII; secolo XVIII; secolo XIX; italiani in Birmania, India, Afganistan Giappone, Malesia; italiani nel Siam; secolo XX; collettività italiana in Giappone e Mancio-Kuo; concessione di Tien Tsin.

Civiltà cristiana in Africa

Limitiamo l'elencazione al solo settore propriamente storico della Mostra, ma non si deve tralasciare di considerare che anche gli altri settori, quello geografico soprattutto, offrivano materiale preziosissimo al di là di un interesse soltanto contingente al momento. Così i singoli padiglioni della Libia, dell'A.O.I., delle Isole Italiane dell'Egeo, dell'Albania presentavano sullo sfondo delle loro realizzazioni architettoniche spettacolari e accanto alla illustrazione dei rispettivi elementi geografici, etnici, folcloristici ed economici, una dettagliata documentazione della preistoria e della storia di quei territori, con speciale riguardo alle relazioni intercorse nei secoli con l'Italia, dai tempi più lontani fino alle realizzazioni colonizzatrici degli ultimi anni. Come pure si deve tenere presente che quello che nel 1940 appariva contingente e a carattere essenzialmente politico, ha ora, dopo tanto precipitare di avvenimenti, esso stesso un valore storico e documentario, di ingente entità, ai fini del particolare significato e della specifica funzione che la Mostra ha ora acquistato ai nostri occhi.

Per questo ci auguriamo che, quali possano essere gli sviluppi pratici della Triennale nell'immediato futuro, sia possibile domani ricostruire per lo meno un dettagliato inventario della Mostra, un ampio catalogo ragionato del materiale raccolto, specialmente di quello documentario, tratto da Archivi, Biblioteche, Istituti, Musei, Collezioni private, e pubbliche d'ogni parte d'Italia e delle Colonie, in modo che se ne possano mantenere unite le disperse fila e consentire con ciò (indipendentemente dalla auspicata ripresa della manifestazione) la possibilità agli studiosi di trarre3 tutti gli insegnamenti che dalla Mostra possono e devono dedursi, nel senso sopra indicato; e sia possibile così continuare e integrare quanto già l'Ente ordinatore si era proposto con l'edizione di tutta una serie di studi monografici d'ampio respiro informati a criteri strettamente scientifici, per la definitiva elaborazione dei dati e risultati offerti della Mostra stessa, nei suoi singoli settori e aspetti:

Inventario e catalogo – questo – che, naturalmente, non si deve confondere con i già pubblicati documentari e guide che, per essere intonati a intendimenti troppo pubblicitari e troppo pratici, non danno che una sommaria e inadeguata visione della Mostra, sottolineandone più che altro il carattere spettacolare e contingente.

È vero sì che la realizzazione della Triennale rappresentò per Napoli e per l'Italia stessa un'opera superba di volontà e di intelligenza e il frutto di un importante complesso di lavoro scientifico, tecnico, artistico, artigiano e operaio che resterà una delle manifestazioni più significative del momento storico.

Ma – ripetiamo – dietro tutta la fantasmagoria dell'incomparabile scenario, al di là del meraviglioso fascino delle forme, delle luci, dei colori, dei suoni coordinati all'esaltazione dell'Idea, questa Idea più ancora si esalta e vive superba nell'evidenza nuda dei dati a cui essi hanno voluto dare espressione appariscente. Questa espressione è caduca.

Quei dati sono eterni, perché rispecchiano la realtà dei fatti e ci indicano la via del nostro divenire.

Faber

La Prima Mostra Triennale delle Terre Italiane d'Oltremare di Napoli (1940) e l'Esposizione Universale di Roma E42 (prevista per il 1942 e mai inaugurata), sono state progettate ed utilizzate, nel ventennio, come strumenti di comunicazione tra masse e potere. Esse possono essere considerate documenti storici complessi ed allo stesso tempo monumenti contenenti insiemi compositi di risorse artistiche, culturali ed ambientali. Sono documenti storico-artistici come insiemi materiali testimoni di un periodo che ha segnato, tra gli anni Trenta e Quaranta del Novecento, grandi avvenimenti per la storia politica d'Italia e dell'Europa, per la storia dell'arte e dell'architettura della città di Napoli e di Roma; e sono pure, in senso etimologico, monumenti come segni che furono posti a ricordo di un avvenimento; come singolari insiemi di opere d'arte, d'architettura, di scultura, di arte figurativa e decorativa, come complessi ambientali e come sistemazioni urbanistiche, modelli significativi di un modo contingente di progettare la città negli anni contesi dal razionalismo e dal ritorno all'ordine. Il volume propone un confronto delle due grandi esposizioni condotto su più piani: istituzionale, evidenziando le tappe principali che ne hanno segnato la nascita; urbanistico ed architettonico, prestando attenzione all'impatto delle due mostre sulla realtà sociale circostante, e quindi museologico, soffermandosi sull'articolazione degli spazi espositivi.

Bibliografia essenziale

ESPOSIZIONI DEL VENTENNIO
PRIMA MOSTRA TRIENNALE DELLE TERRE ITALIANE D'OLTREMARE
ESPOSIZIONE UNIVERSALE DI ROMA E42

1929
MUSSOLINI, B., *Roma antica sul mare*, Mantova 1929.

1933
Campana, M., *L'impero fascista*, Firenze 1933.

1934
CAMPANA, E., *L'Italia alla II Mostra Internazionale Coloniale nel Maschio Angioino di Napoli*, in «Emporium», vol. LXXX, n. 478, ottobre, Bergamo 1934, p. 242.
MARINETTI, F.T., *Gli aeropittori futuristi italiani alla Mostra Coloniale di Napoli*, in ENTE AUTONOMO FIERA CAMPIONARIA DI TRIPOLI (a cura di), *Seconda Mostra Internazionale d'Arte Coloniale, Napoli 1934-XII-1935-XIII. Catalogo*, catalogo della mostra, (Napoli, Castelnuovo, 1 ottobre 1934- 31 gennaio 1935), Roma 1934, p. 42.

1935
TADDEINI, O. I., MERCANTE, L., *Arte fascista. Arte per la massa*, Roma 1935.

1936
AA.VV., *Il nuovo stile littorio. I progetti per il Palazzo del Littorio e della Mostra della Rivoluzione Fascista in Via dell'Impero*, Milano-Roma 1936.
D'AMBROSIO, G., *Il Duce e l'Impero. Invicta Roma Aeterna*, Napoli 1936.
LEVI, M.A., *La politica imperiale di Roma*, Torino 1936.

1937
Il Piano regolatore dell'Esposizione Universale di Roma 1941-1942 (architetti G. Pagano, M. Piacentini, L. Piccinato, E. Rossi, L. Vietti), in «Casabella», a. X, n. 114, giugno 1937, p. 4-15.
SAPORI, F., *Storia dell'arte e tutela del patrimonio artistico nell'Italia fascista*, Roma 1937.

1938
BOTTAI, G., *Discorso pronunziato al convegno dei Soprintendenti alle Antichità e Belle Arti*, in «Bollettino d'Arte», a. XXXII, luglio 1938, pp. 1-9.
CALZA, G., *Rassegna dell'antico turismo romano alla Mostra Augustea*, in «Le Vie d'Italia», a. XLIV, n. 2, febbraio, Milano 1938, pp. 161-167
L'Esposizione Universale di Roma 1942, in «Architettura», fascicolo speciale, dicembre 1938
PAIS, E., *Roma dall'antico al nuovo impero*, Milano 1938.
QUIVIS, *L'Esposizione Universale di Roma*, in «Le Vie d'Italia», a. XLIV, n. 4, aprile, Milano 1938, pp. 419-426.
RAVA, M., *Mussolini fondatore dell'Impero*, in GIORDANO, M., *L'Impero Coloniale Fascista*, Novara 1938, pp. 17-20.
STOCCHETTI, F., *La Triennale d'Oltremare*, in «Le Vie d'Italia», a. XLIV, n. 7, luglio, Milano 1938, pp. 832-836.

1939
CINI V., *Invito*, in *Esposizione Universale di Roma. MCMXLII-ANNO XX° E.F.*, a cura del Commissariato Generale, Roma 1939, pp. 17-20.
COBOLLI GIGLI, G., *Il contributo del Ministero dei Lavori Pubblici al piano regolatore di Roma imperiale*, Roma 1939, pp. 16-17.

DE LILLO, L., *Napoli nel clima dell'impero. Sorge la Triennale d'Oltremare*, in «L'illustrazione Italiana», a. LXVII, n. 34, 20 agosto, Milano 1939, pp. 319-324.
GIOVANNONI, G., *Lineamenti fondamentali del piano regolatore di Roma imperiale*, Roma 1939, pp. 7-8.
L'E42 in Roma: stato dei lavori e nuovi progetti. Le sistemazioni urbanistiche connesse: via Imperiale e nuova stazione di Roma Termini, in «Architettura», fascicolo speciale, dicembre 1939.

1940
AA.VV., *Prima Mostra Triennale delle Terre Italiane d'Oltremare, Napoli 9 maggio-15 ottobre 1940 XVIII. Documentario*, Napoli 1940.
BIANCALE, M., *La prima Mostra Triennale delle terre italiane d'Oltremare*, in «Le Arti», a. IIII, fasc. I, ottobre-novembre, Firenze 1940, pp. 54-57.
BERNARD, C., *Triennale d'Oltremare*, in «Tempo», a. IV, n. 53, numero speciale sulla Triennale d'Oltremare, 30 maggio 1940, pp. 21-22.
BOTTAI, G., *Discorso per la inaugurazione della VII Triennale a Milano*, in «Le Arti», a. II, fasc. IV, aprile-maggio 1940, pp. 221-222.
- *Politica fascista delle arti*, Roma 1940.
- *Come si delinea la Mostra Triennale delle Terre d'Oltremare*, in «Il Lavoro Fascista», Roma 4 gennaio 1940.
CINI, V., *Significato e aspetti dell'esposizione universale di Roma*, in «Civiltà», aprile 1940.
COCCHIA, C., *Architettura del verde e fontane alla Triennale d'Oltremare*, Napoli 1940.
CONTADINO, M., *Un immenso cantiere sui Campi Flegrei. Sorge la prima Mostra delle terre italiane d'oltremare*, in «Il Lavoro Fascista», Roma 31 gennaio 1940.
DELL'ERBA, F., *Alla Triennale d'Oltremare i Missionari italiani in Africa*, in «Il Giornale d'Italia», Roma, 6 febbraio 1940.
- *La Triennale delle Terre d'Oltremare*, in «Il Giornale d'Italia», Roma 28 febbraio 1940.
- *L'arte antica alla "Triennale"*, in «Il Giornale d'Italia», Roma 8 marzo 1940.
- *Morelli e i pittori orientalisti alla Triennale d'Oltremare*, in «Il Giornale d'Italia», Roma 5 aprile 1940.
DE LILLO, L., *Potenza imperiale dell'Italia fascista nei riflessi della Prima Mostra delle Terre d'Oltremare*, in «L'Illustrazione Italiana», a. LXVII, n. 4, 28 gennaio, Milano 1940, pp. 103-106.
DE LUCA, G., *Problemi del Teatro di massa*, Roma 1940.
«Emporium», a. XLVI, n. 548, agosto, Bergamo 1940, interamente dedicato alla *Prima Mostra delle Terre Italiane d'Oltremare.*
ENTE AUTONOMO TRIENNALE D'OLTREMARE (a cura di), *I Mostra Triennale delle Terre Italiane d'Oltremare. Napoli 9 maggio–15 ottobre 1940-XVIII. Guida*, Napoli 1940.
«Etiopia. Rassegna illustrata dell'Impero», a. IV, n. 5, Roma 1940, p. 16.
GENTILE, G., *Arte contemporanea*, in «Le Arti», a. II, fascicolo III, febbraio-marzo 1940, pp. 142-145.
La grande esedra a giochi d'acqua alla Triennale d'Oltremare, in «Il Giornale d'Italia», Roma 27 gennaio 1940.
La Mostra d'Arte dei G.U.F., in «Il Lavoro Fascista», Roma 5 gennaio 1940.
LA REDAZIONE, *Per l'Arte contemporanea*, in «Le Arti», a. II, fascicolo III, febbraio-marzo 1940, pp. 140-141.
Le isole dell'Egeo alla Triennale, in «Il Giornale d'Italia», Roma 14 gennaio 1940.
«L'illustrazione Italiana», a. LXVII, n. 22, 2 giugno, numero speciale dedicato alla Mostra Triennale delle Terre d'Oltremare, Milano 1940.
L'Ufficio per l'Arte Contemporanea, in «Le Arti», a. II, fasc. III, febbraio-marzo, Firenze 1940.
MAIURI, A., *Il segno di Roma alla Mostra delle Terre d'Oltremare*, in «L'illustrazione Italiana», a. LXVII, n. 22, 2 giugno, numero speciale dedicato alla Mostra Triennale delle Terre d'Oltremare, Milano 1940, pp. 807-810.
MARCONI. P., *Il quartiere dell'E42 fulcro del Piano regolatore di Roma Imperiale*, Roma 1940.
MASELLI, E., *Pittura e scultura alla Triennale d'Oltremare*, in «Il lavoro Fascista», Roma 10 maggio 1940.
«Napoli. Rivista municipale», nn. 4-5, aprile-maggio, Napoli 1940.
POZZI, A., *Orme di legionari sulle Terre d'Oltremare*, in «Le Vie d'Italia», a. XLVI, n. 6, giugno, Milano 1940, pp. 601-614.

SOLARIANO, *Alla vigilia della inaugurazione della Mostra d'Oltremare. Un tipico aspetto della Triennale*, in «Il Lavoro Fascista», Roma 8 maggio 1940.
«Tempo», a. IV, n. 53, numero speciale sulla Triennale d'Oltremare, 30 maggio 1940.
TRIDENTI C., *La Direzione delle Arti e l'ufficio per l'Arte Contemporanea (colloquio con Marino Lazzari)*, in «Il Giornale d'Italia», Roma 12 gennaio 1940.
Una città nuova sorge ai margini dei Campi Flegrei, in «Il Lavoro Fascista», Roma 11 gennaio 1940.

1941
«Architettura», nn. 1-2, gennaio-febbraio 1941, numero doppio monografico dedicato alla *Prima Mostra Triennale delle Terre Italiane d'Oltremare*, Milano 1941.
COCCHIA, C., *I Ristoranti alla Triennale di Napoli*, in «L'Architettura Italiana», ottobre, Torino 1941, pp. 297-314.
DEI GASLINI, M., *Il Governo dei Galla e Sidama alla Mostra Triennale d'Oltremare*, Bergamo 1941.
ENTE AUTONOMO MOSTRA D'OLTREMARE (a cura di), *I Mostra Triennale delle Terre Italiane d'Oltremare. Guida*, Napoli 1941.
«Etiopia. Rassegna illustrata dell'Impero», numero speciale sulla Triennale d'Oltremare, Roma 1941.
LIBERA, A., *I mosaici del palazzo dei ricevimenti all'Esposizione Universale*, in«Civiltà», n. 5, 21 aprile 1941.
MOLAJOLI, B., DE FILIPPIS F. (a cura di), *La mostra d'Arte retrospettiva alla Triennale d'Oltremare. Catalogo*, Napoli 1941.
OPPO, C.E., *La chiesa dei SS. Pietro e Paolo all'Esposizione*, in «Civiltà», n. 4, 21 gennaio 1941.
ORTOLANI, S., MOLAJOLI, F., DE FILIPPIS, F. (a cura di), *Le Terre d'Oltremare e l'Arte italiana dal Quattrocento all'Ottocento*, Napoli 1941.
ORTONA, U., *Le Terre d'Oltremare e l'Arte italiana Contemporanea*, catalogo della mostra, Napoli 1941.
PICCINATO, L., *Stucchi*, in «Cellini», a. II, n. 6, 1941, p. 6.
Roma antica sul mare, in «Etiopia. Rassegna illustrata dell'Impero», numero speciale sulla Triennale d'Oltremare, Roma 1941, pp. 19-21.

1942
Il Padiglione Cultura Propaganda e Sanità alla Mostra Triennale delle Terre d'Oltremare a Napoli. Arch. Ferdinando Chiaromonte, in «Architettura Italiana», aprile-maggio, Torino 1942, pp. 82-84.

1947
DE CESARE, S., *Un progetto sulla Mostra d'Oltremare*, in «L'illustrazione del Sud», n. 2, aprile 1947, p. 12.

1950
Fiera di Napoli e Mostra d'Oltremare, in «Il Mercantile», Napoli 29 ottobre 1950.
LEFEVRE, L., *Risorge la Mostra d'Oltremare. L'attività dell'Ente per la ripresa delle sue finalità e per la valorizzazione del suo imponente complesso monumentale e documentario*, in «Il Giornale del mezzogiorno», 23 ottobre 1950.
LOVERO, N., *Triste destino della Mostra d'Oltremare. Dalla Mostra dell'imperialismo di cartapesta alle celebrazioni servili dell'ERP e del dollaro*, in «L'Unità», 21 ottobre 1950.
«Oltremare. Rassegna mensile dell'Ente autonomo Mostra d'oltremare e del lavoro italiano nel mondo», a. I, n. 1, ottobre 1950.
«Oltremare. Rassegna mensile dell'Ente autonomo Mostra d'oltremare e del lavoro italiano nel mondo», a. I, n. 3, dicembre 1950.
RUSSO, G., *Il testamento di una statua*, in «Oltremare», a. I, n. 3, dicembre, Napoli 1950, pp. 13-14.

1951
LOCCHI, G.Z., *Napoli 1951. rivive in un nuovo destino la Mostra d'Oltremare*, in «La Patria degli Italiani», 30 dicembre 1951.

1952
AA.VV., *I Mostra Triennale del Lavoro Italiano nel Mondo. Guida*, Torino 1952.

BOLOGNA, F., CAUSA, R., *Fontainebleau e la Maniera Italiana*, catalogo della mostra, (Napoli, Mostra d'Oltremare e del Lavoro Italiano nel Mondo, 26 luglio-12 ottobre 1952), Firenze 1952.
Fiore, E. (a cura di), *I Mostra Triennale del Lavoro Italiano nel Mondo*, catalogo della mostra (Napoli, Mostra d'Oltremare e del Lavoro Italiano nel Mondo, giugno-ottobre 1952), Napoli 1952.
RUSSO, G., *La Mostra d'Oltremare*, Napoli 1952.

1953
CARNELLI, F., FIORE, E. (a cura di), *Ente Autonomo Mostra d'Oltremare e del Lavoro Italiano nel mondo - Napoli. Manifestazioni 1953*, Napoli 1953.
COCCHIA, C., *La Mostra d'Oltremare*, in «Urbanistica», rivista della Sezione Regionale piemontese dell'Istituto Nazionale di Urbanistica, nn. 10-11, Roma 1953.
SAPORI, F., *Architettura in roma 1901-1950*, Roma 1953.

1954
RICCIO, S., *La Mostra d'Oltremare e la sua ricostruzione*, Roma 1954.

1955
COCCHIA, C., *Mostra d'Oltremare a Napoli*, in «L'Architettura. Cronache e Storia», n. 2, luglio-agosto, Roma 1955.

1956
CANINO, E., *Clotilde tra le due guerre*, Milano 1956.

1958
COCCHIA, C., *Due Regolamenti Edilizi per la città di Napoli: 1886 e 1935*, Napoli 1958.

1959
AA.VV., *Roma città e piani*, numero monografico di «Urbanistica», Torino 1959, pp. 164-168.
Per la Triennale d'Oltremare, in SUSMEL, D., SUSMEL, E. (a cura di), *Opera omnia di Benito Mussolini*, vol. XXIX, Firenze 1959, p. 112.

1961
COCCHIA, C., *L'edilizia a Napoli dal 1918 al 1958*, Napoli 1961.

1967
BREGLIA, L., *Numismatica antica. Storia e metodologia*, 1967.

1968
PRETI, L., *Impero fascista, africani ed ebrei*, Milano 1968.
1970
CANNISTRARO , P. V., *Burocrazia e politica culturale nello stato fascista: il Ministero della Cultura Popolare*, estratto da «Storia contemporanea», a. I, n. 2, Bologna 1970, pp. 273-298.

1971
DE POLIS S., RAVAGLIOLI A., *La Terza Roma*, Roma 1971, pp. 41-45.

1972
ARMELLINI, G., *Fascismo e pittura italiana*, in «Paragone», n. 273, novembre, Firenze 1972, pp. 37-51.
DE ANTONELLIS, G., *Napoli sotto il Regime. Storia di una città e della sua regione durante il ventennio fascista*, Milano 1972
DE SETA, C. (a cura di), *La cultura architettonica in Italia tra le due guerre*, Bari 1972

1973

D'ONOFRIO, C., *Renovatio Romae*, Roma 1973, pp. 220-259.
GHIRELLI A., *Storia di Napoli*, Torino 1973.
SILVA U., *Ideologia e arte del fascismo*, Milano 1973.

1974
RAGGHIANTI C.L., RECUPERO J., *Ferruccio Ferrazzi*, Roma 1974.

1975
GHIRELLI A., *Napoli Sbagliata. Storia della città tra le due guerre*, Napoli 1975.
CANNISTRARO, P., *La fabbrica del consenso. Fascismo e mass media*, Roma-Bari 1975
1976
CAGNETTA M., *Il mito di Augusto e la rivoluzione fascista*, in «Quaderni di storia 3», 1976, pp. 139-181.
DANESI, S., PATETTA, L. (a cura di), *Il razionalismo e l'architettura in Italia durante il Fascismo*, Venezia 1976.
TEMPESTI, F., *Arte dell'Italia fascista*, Milano 1976.

1977
PERELLI, L., *Sul culto fascista della romanità*, in «Quaderni di storia 5», 1977, pp. 197-224.

1978
GALASSO, G., *Intervista sulla storia di Napoli*, Bari 1978.
LE GOFF, J., *Documento/Monumento*, in *Enciclopedia*, vol. V, Torino 1978, p. 38.
PANSERA, A., *Storia e cronaca della Triennale*, Milano 1978.
SANFILIPPO, M., *Le città, il fascismo*, Roma 1978.

1979
CEDERNA, A., *Mussolini urbanista: Lo sventramento di Roma negli anni del consenso*, Roma-Bari 1979.
BRASINI, L., (a cura di), *L'opera architettonica e urbanistica di Armando Brasini*, Roma 1979.
CAGNETTA, M., *Antichisti e impero fascista*, Bari 1979.
DEL BOCA, A., *Gli italiani in Africa Orientale. La conquista dell'Impero*, tomo II, Roma-Bari 1979.
FOLIN, A., (a cura di), *Immagine di popolo e organizzazione del consenso in Italia negli anni Trenta e Quaranta*, catalogo della mostra, (Venezia, Museo d'Arte Moderna Ca' Pesaro, novembre-dicembre 1979), Venezia 1979.
ISNEGHI, M., *L'educazione dell'italiano: il fascismo e l'organizzazione della cultura*, Bologna 1979.

1980
GRECO, E. (a cura di), *La Mostra d'Oltremare dalle origini al 1980*, Napoli 1980.
LAVAGGI, S., FICO C., POLITO S., *Fuorigrotta e Bagnoli*, collana «I quartieri di Napoli. Cronaca e documenti 1860-1940», Napoli 1980.
MOSSE, G. L., *Masse and Man. Nationalist and Fascist*, New York 1980.
VENERUSO, D., *L'Italia fascista 1922-1945*, Bologna 1980.

1981
BENEVOLO, L., *Storia dell'architettura moderna*, Bari 1981.
COCCHIA, C., *Da un vicolo di Napoli alla Mostra d'Oltremare*, in AA.VV., *Lo spazio della città. Trasformazioni urbane a Napoli nell'ultimo secolo*, Napoli 1981, pp. 16-29.
- *L'espansione della città moderna, Napoli 1940: nella proiezione d'Oltremare*, in «Hinterland», a. IV, nn. 19-20, Milano 1981.

DE SETA, C., *L'architettura del novecento*, Torino 1981

RICCI P., *La fabbrica ceramica di Posillipo*, in *Arte e Artisti a Napoli (1800-1943). Cronache e memorie di Paolo Ricci*, Napoli 1981, pp. 225-226.
1982

GENTILE E., *Il mito dello stato nuovo dall'antigiolittismo al fascismo*, Roma-Bari 1982.
1984
BORRELLI G., *Un poeta della scultura maiolicata. Giuseppe Macedonio*, in «Realtà del Mezzogiorno», n. 10, Roma 1984, pp. 758-759.
MIGNEMI, A. (a cura di), *Immagine coordinata per un impero. Etiopia 1935 – 1936*, Novara 1984.

1985
COEN, E., LUX, S. (a cura di), *1935: gli artisti nell'università e la questione della pittura murale*, catalogo della mostra, (Università degli Studi di Roma «La Sapienza» 1985), Roma 1985.
MUNTONI, A., *Via dell'Impero tra "Forma Urbis" e piano della grande Roma*, in «Parametro», n. 138, luglio 1985, Bologna-Faenza 1985, pp. 31-42.

1986
BORRELLI G., *Giuseppe Macedonio ceramista e scultore*, in «Napoli Nobilissima», fasc. III-IV, maggio-agosto 1986, pp. 137-141.
BRANCACCIO L., *Carlo Farneti*, in PICONE PETRUSA M. (a cura di), *In margine. Artisti napoletani fra tradizione e opposizione. 1909-1923*, catalogo della mostra, Milano 1986, pp. 179-185.
CASAVECCHIA M. (a cura di), *E. B. Lapadula. Opere e scritti 1930-1949*, Venezia 1986.
INSOLERA I., DI MAIO L., *L'EUR a Roma dagli anni Trenta al Duemila*, Roma-Bari 1986.
PICONE PETRUSA M. (a cura di), *In margine. Artisti napoletani fra tradizione e opposizione. 1909-1923*, catalogo della mostra, Milano 1986.
PINTO V., *Iconografie Ceramiche Vietresi*, Salerno 1986.

1987
CALVESI, M., GUIDONI, E., LUX, S. (a cura di), *E 42. Utopia e scenario del Regime*, vol. II, *Urbanistica, architettura, arte e decorazione*, Venezia 1987
CASTONOVO, V., *La città italiana dell'economia corporativa*, in GREGORY, T., TARTARO, A. (a cura di), *E 42. Utopia e scenario del Regime*, vol. I, *Ideologia e programma dell'Olimpiade della Civiltà*, Venezia 1987, pp. 17-25
GALASSO, G. (a cura di), *Napoli*, collana «Storia delle città italiane», Bari 1987
GANGEMI, V., *Sul rapporto fra architettura e decorazione*, in «Rassegna semestrale del Dipartimento di Configurazione e Attuazione dell'Architettura», a. I, n 2, dicembre 1987, pp. 36-39
GARIN, E., *La Civiltà italiana nell'esposizione del 1942*, in GREGORY, T., TARTARO, A. (a cura di), *E 42. Utopia e scenario del Regime*, vol. I, *Ideologia e programma dell'Olimpiade della Civiltà*, Venezia 1987, pp. 3-16
GODOLI, E., *L'E 42 e le esposizioni universali*, in CALVESI, M., GUIDONI, E., LUX, S. (a cura di), *E 42. Utopia e scenario del Regime*, vol. II, *Urbanistica, architettura, arte e decorazione*, Venezia 1987, pp. 147-155
GREGORY, T., TARTARO, A. (a cura di), *E 42. Utopia e scenario del Regime*, vol. I, *Ideologia e programma dell'Olimpiade della Civiltà*, Venezia 1987
GUIDONI, E., *L'E 42, città della rappresentazione. Il progetto urbanistico e le polemiche sull'architettura*, , in CALVESI, M., GUIDONI, E., LUX, S. (a cura di), *E 42. Utopia e scenario del Regime*, vol. II, *Urbanistica, architettura, arte e decorazione*, Venezia 1987, pp. 19-20
MARIANI, R., *E 42: un progetto per l'ordine nuovo*, Milano 1987
1988
CRISPOLTI, E., *La politica culturale del fascismo, le avanguardie e il problema del futurismo*, in DE FELICE, R. (a cura di), *Futurismo. Cultura e Politica*, Torino 1988, pp. 247-283.
DE VICO FALLANI, M., *Parchi e giardini dell'Eur*, Roma 1988.
MALVANO L., *Fascismo e politica dell'immagine*, Torino 1988.
NAPOLITANO G., *Triennale d'Oltremare: una suggestiva sintesi ceramica-architettura*, in «Quaderni Centro Studi per la ceramica meridionale», Napoli 1988, pp. 33-34.

1989

CIUCCI, G., *Gli architetti italiani e il fascismo, architettura e città 1922-1942*, Torino 1989.
HULTEN, P., CELANT, G. (a cura di), *Arte Italiana. Presenze 1900-1945*, catalogo della mostra, (Venezia, Palazzo Grassi 1989), Milano 1989
LANARO, S., *Un regime fra le due guerre*, in HULTEN, P., CELANT, G. (a cura di), *Arte Italiana. Presenze 1900-1945*, catalogo della mostra, (Venezia, Palazzo Grassi 1989), Milano 1989, pp. 121-134
LIPOVETSKY, G., *L'impero dell'effimero*, Milano 1989
MAGNAGO LAMPUGNANI, V., *Architettura, pittura e arte decorativa in Italia: 1923-1940, dalla I Biennale alla VII Triennale*, in HULTEN, P., CELANT, G. (a cura di), *Arte Italiana. Presenze 1900-1945*, catalogo della mostra, (Venezia, Palazzo Grassi 1989), Milano 1989, pp. 69-76
MARAINI, R., *Razionalismo e architettura moderna. Storia di una polemica*, Milano 1989

1990
BARONI D., *Grafica e propaganda. La Mostra d'Oltremare del 1940*, in «ArQ», n. 3, giugno 1990, Roma 1990, pp. 85-88.
CAPOBIANCO M., *Marcello Canino tra le due guerre o della modernità inattuale*, in «ArQ», n. 3, giugno 1990, Roma 1990, pp. 7-38.
DE FEO KEMPF C.M., *Le serre botaniche tropicali di Carlo Cocchia*, in «ArQ», n. 3, giugno 1990, Roma 1990, pp. 89-91.
DI MAJO, L., *L'E42 e l'autocelebrazione del regime*, in AA.VV., *Il Parlamento italiano 1861-1988. Storia Parlamentare e politica dell'Italia*, vol. XII, tomo II, *1939-1945. Dal «consenso» al crollo: dalla II guerra mondiale alla liberazione*, Milano 1990, pp. 54-58

GIORDANO P., *Area Occidentale: la direttrice Fuorigrotta/Bagnoli*, in SIOLA U., MAGNAGO LAMPUGNANI V. (a cura di), *Napoli. Architettura e città*, I Seminario Internazionale di progettazione, (Napoli, Castel Sant'Elmo, 28 agosto-16 settembre 1989), Milano 1990, pp. 76-80.
- *Area occidentale: la Mostra d'Oltremare*, in GIORDANO, P. (a cura di), *Napoli. Architettura e città*, II Seminario Internazionale di progettazione, Napoli 1990, pp. 98-111.
GOLOMSTOCK I., *Totalitarian Art in the Soviet Union, the Third Reich, fascist Italy and the People's Republic of China*, London 1990.
GUZZI, D., *2% considerazioni in margine*, Roma 1990.
IZZO F., *Dal teatro classico al teatro di massa. L'Arena Flegrea*, in «ArQ», n. 3, giugno 1990, Roma 1990, pp. 92-94.
LUX S., MURATORE, G., (a cura di), *Palazzo dei Congressi*, Roma 1990.
MARIANI, R., *LA progettazione dell'E42, Prima fase*, in «Lotus», n. 67, 1990, pp. 90-126.
MUNTONI, A., *Esposizioni e regime, ideologie e colonialismo, e Roma 1942, L'Esposizione Universale*, in «Quaderni DI», n. 11, pp 61-70 e 175-180.
PIGNATTI MORANO M., DI SANTO N., REFICE P. (a cura di), *E42 l'immagine ritrovata. Catalogo dei cartoni e degli studi per la decorazione*, Roma 1990.
PULEO A.M., *Piano Regolatore e progetti architettonici nella Mostra Triennale delle Terre Italiane d'Oltremare*, in «ArQ», n. 3, giugno 1990, Roma 1990, pp. 74-84.
SIOLA U., *La Mostra d'Oltremare e Fuorigrotta*, Napoli 1990.
VARVARO P., *Una città fascista. Potere e società a Napoli*, Palermo 1990.
1991
ABRUZZESE, A., *Estetiche del conflitto e del potere*, in «Quaderni Di», n. 11, Napoli 1991, pp. 13-26.

BORRELLI G., *1940. Mostra delle Terre Italiane d'Oltremare. Belle Arti*, in «Quaderni Di», n. 11, Napoli 1991, pp. 171-174.
DE LUCA G., *L'Arena Flegrea: cronaca di 50 anni raccontata dall'autore*, in «Costruttiva», a. 2, n. 12, dicembre, Napoli 1991, pp. 5-7.
D'AGOSTINO G., *Napoli dal dopoguerra agli anni Sessanta. Società, elezioni e governo locale*, in PICONE PETRUSA M. (a cura di), *Fuori dall'ombra. Nuove tendenze nelle arti a Napoli dal '45 al '65*, catalogo della mostra, (Napoli, Castel Sant'Elmo, 9 novembre 1991-19 gennaio 1992),

Napoli 1991, pp. 21-30.
LA REDAZIONE, *1940 Prima Triennale delle Terre Italiane d'Oltremare*, in «Quaderni Di», n. 11, Napoli 1991, pp. 165-170.
MASI, A., *Un'arte per lo stato: dalla nascita della metafisica alla Legge del 2%*, Napoli 1991.
MUNTONI A., *Esposizioni e regime: ideologia e colonialismo, l'E.42 e la Mostra d'Oltremare*, in «Quaderni Di», n. 11, Napoli 1991, pp. 61-70.
PICONE PETRUSA M., *L'arte nel Mezzogiorno d'Italia dall'Unità alla seconda guerra mondiale*, in GALASSO G., ROMEO R. (a cura di), *Storia del Mezzogiorno*, vol. XIV, Napoli 1991, pp. 89-91.
RICCI G., *La cultura architettonica a Napoli dal 1945 al 1965*, in PICONE PETRUSA M., *Fuori dall'ombra. Nuove tendenze nelle arti a Napoli dal '45 al '65*, catalogo della mostra, (Napoli, Castel Sant'Elmo, 9 novembre 1991-19 gennaio 1992, Napoli 1991, pp. 523-532.
1992
DORE G., *Ideologia coloniale e senso comune etnografico nella Mostra delle terre italiane d'Oltremare*, in LABANCA N. (a cura di), *L'Africa in vetrina. Storie di musei e di esposizioni coloniali in Italia*, Treviso 1992, pp. 47-65.
INTARTAGLIA C, SCARAMELLA C. (a cura di), *Archivio Storico della Società Africana d'Italia. Inventario*, vol. I, Napoli 1992.
1993
GENTILE E., *Il culto del littorio*, Roma-Bari 1993.
STONE M., *Staging Fascism: The Exhibition of the Fascist Revolution*, in «Journal of Contemporary History 28/2», 1993, pp. 215-243.
1994
AA.VV., *La Mostra d'Oltremare*, in LEBRO D., LEBRO M., NOVELLI I. (a cura di), *L'immediato possibile. Un ponte tra l'impossibile ed il possibile in 16 idee-progetto per la città di Napoli*, Napoli 1994, pp. 135-139.
BELFIORE P., GRAVAGNUOLO B., *Napoli. Architettura e urbanistica del Novecento*, Bari 1994, pp. 209-216.
CEFARIELLO GROSSO G., *La produzione vietrese nel rinnovamento della ceramica italiana tra le due guerre*, in ROMITO M. (a cura di), *Il Museo della Ceramica. Raito di Vietri sul Mare*, catalogo, Salerno 1994, pp. 85-89.
CUCCU A., *La moderna ceramica vietrese tra progetto colto e artigianato*, in ROMITO M. (a cura di), *Il Museo della Ceramica. Raito di Vietri sul Mare*, catalogo, Salerno 1994, pp. 129-144.
DE FUSCO R., *Napoli nel Novecento*, Napoli 1994.
GIORDANO P., *Napoli. Guida di Architettura Moderna*, Roma 1994, pp. 36-73.
GRAVAGNUOLO B. (a cura di), *Napoli, il porto e la città. Storia e progetti*, Napoli 1994.
PAPA, E. R., *Bottai e l'arte: un fascismo diverso? La politica culturale di Giuseppe Bottai e il Premio Bergamo (1939-1942)*, Milano 1994.
1995
CORVINO V., LANINI L., *Il restauro della Torre delle Nazioni*, Napoli 1995.
MUNTONI, A., *La videnda dell'E42. Fondazione di una città in forma didascalica*, in CIUCCI, G., *Classicismo/Classicismi, Quaderni di Architettura*, Milano 1995, pp. 128-143.
SIRONI, M., *Manifesto della pittura Murale*, in «La Colonna», dicembre 1933, riprodotto in BOSSAGLIA, R., *Il Novecento Italiano*, Milano 1995, pp. 155-157.
STURANI, E., *Otto milioni di cartoline per il Duce*, Torino 1995.

1996
CAPOBIANCO M., *Le ceneri dell'impegno*, in «ArQ», n. 11, dicembre 1993, Napoli 1996, pp. 97-142.
COLONNESI D., *l'architettura di Vittorio Amicarelli alla Mostra d'Oltremare di Napoli*, Napoli 1996.
CRISPOLTI E., *Nella Fiera del Levante a Bari, 1935, e nella Mostra d'Oltremare a Napoli, 1940*, in CRISPOLTI E. (a cura di), *Futurismo e Meridione*, catalogo della mostra, (Napoli, Palazzo Reale, 18 luglio-31 ottobre 1996), Napoli 1996, pp. 235-243.
DAL PIAZ, A., MESOLELLA, A., *L'urbanistica in Italia nel Novecento*, in «ArQ», n. 12, *Architettura italiana 1920-1939*, giugno 1994, Napoli 1996, pp. 45-71.
D'AMBROSIO M., *Carlo Cocchia*, in CRISPOLTI E. (a cura di), *Futurismo e Meridione*, catalogo della mostra, (Napoli, Palazzo Reale, 18 luglio-31 ottobre 1996), Napoli 1996, p. 467.

ENTE AUTONOMO ESPOSIZIONE UNIVERSALE DI ROMA (a cura di), *Leggi, decreti e provvedimenti: 1936-1996*, Roma 1996.
ORLACCHIO D., *Il dibattito urbanistico e il Piano del '39*, in «I Quaderni de il Cerchio», n. 1, *La Ricerca dello Stato nuovo*, Napoli 1996, pp. 63-74.
QUILICI, V., *E42 EUR. Un centro per la metropoli*, Roma 1996.
ROSSI, P. O., *Caratteri stilistici nell'architettura di Roma degli anni Venti. Quale strada per uscire dall'eclettismo?*, in «ArQ», n. 11, dicembre 1993, Napoli 1996, pp. 41-62.

PALMA S. (a cura di), *Archivio Storico della Società Africana d'Italia. Raccolte fotografiche e cartografiche*, vol. II, Napoli 1996.
RAVAGLIOLI A., *La Roma di Mussolini. Fasti e nefasti del regime fascista nella storia della capitale*, Roma 1996.

1997
DE ANGELIS, D., *Il sindacato belle arti*, in AA.VV., *Arte e Stato. Le esposizioni sindacali nelle Tre Venezie*, catalogo della mostra, (Trieste, Civico Museo Revoltella, 8 marzo – 18 maggio 1997), Milano 1997, pp. 21-30.
ORLACCHIO D., *Il dibattito urbanistico e il Piano del '39*, in «I Quaderni de il Cerchio», n. 2, *La Ricerca dello Stato nuovo. Napoli: Urbanistica e Architettura del Ventennio*, Napoli 1997, pp. 88-102.
PINTO V., *Giovannino ceramista vietrese*, Salerno 1997.
GRIMELLINI C., *La Mostra Triennale delle Terre Italiane d'Oltremare, i Professionisti Napoletani ed i Concorsi di Architettura*, in ROSI M. (a cura di), *Sirio Giammetta. Una testimonianza*, Napoli 1997, pp. 53-75.
TELLINI E. (a cura di), *La Mostra d'Oltremare. Immagini di sessanta anni di storia*, Napoli 1997.
1998
BELFIORE P., *A Oriente e a Occidente di Napoli nel 1952. La rinascita della Mostra dopo la guerra*, in «ArQ», nn. 14-15, giugno-dicembre 1996, Napoli 1998, pp. 257-264.
CAPOBIANCO M., *La polemica su Piazzale Tecchio*, in «ArQ», nn. 14-15, giugno-dicembre 1996, Napoli 1998, pp. 254-256.
CAPOBIANCO M., *Prima Mostra Triennale delle Terre Italiane d'Oltremare. Documentario*, in «ArQ», nn. 14-15, giugno-dicembre 1996, Napoli 1998, pp. 212-253.
DE SETA C. (a cura di), *La cultura architettonica in Italia tra le due guerre*, Napoli 1998.
MAMONE CAPRIA P., *Edoardo Giordano*, Napoli 1998, pp. 26-32.
- *La vicenda figurativa di Edoardo Giordano*, in «ON. OttoNovecento», n. 1, Napoli 1998, pp. 25-36.
PAGANO L., *Mostra d'Oltremare. Un parco urbano*, in CAPPIELLO V., STENTI S. (a cura di) *Napoli Guida. 14 itinerari di architettura moderna*, Napoli 1998, pp. 116-130.
1999
DE SETA C. (a cura di), *L'architettura a Napoli tra le due guerre*, catalogo della mostra, (Napoli, Palazzo Reale, 26 marzo-26 giugno 1999), Napoli 1999.
FAGONE, V., GINEX, G., SPARAGNI, T. (a cura di), *Muri ai pittori. Pittura murale e decorazione in Italia 1930-1950*, catalogo della mostra, (Milano, Museo della Permanente, 16 ottobre 1999 – 3 gennaio 2000), Milano 1999.
FRANZONE G., *Per un'analisi del "ruralesimo" nella Collezione Wolfson. Da Cambellotti alla "mistica rurale" fascista*, in BARISIONE S., FOCHESSATI M., FRANZONE G. (a cura di), *La visione del prisma. La Collezione Wolfson*, catalogo della mostra, (Parma, Voltoni del Guazzatolo, Palazzo Pilotta, 21 novembre 1999-13 febbraio 2000), Milano 1999, pp. 65-91.
MASI, A., *Giuseppe Bottai. La politica delle arti, scritti 1918 – 1943*, Roma 1999.
NICOLOSO, P., *Gli architetti di Mussolini. Scuole e sindacato, architetti e massoni, professori e politici negli anni del regime*, Milano 1999.

PAGANO L., PICCIONI IGNORATO C., STEFANELLI R., *Mostra d'Oltremare. Il mito esotico del quartiere flegreo*, in AA.VV., *Parchi e giardini di Napoli*, Napoli 1999, pp. 125-135.
RUSSO A., *Il fascismo in mostra*, Roma 1999.
2000

DE MARCO P., *Napoli negli anni del fascismo e della guerra*, in PICONE PETRUSA M. (a cura di), *Gli anni difficili. Arte a Napoli dal 1920 al 1945*, catalogo della mostra, (Napoli, Castelnuovo, 28 ottobre-5 dicembre 2000; Villa Pignatelli, 28 ottobre-3 dicembre 2000), Napoli 2000, pp. 17-24.
DE MICHELI, M., *L'arte sotto le dittature*, Milano 2000.
MENNA G., *Vittorio Amicarelli architetto. 1907-1971*, Napoli 2000, pp. 39-50.
POLANO, S., *Mostrare. L'allestimento in Italia dagli anni Venti agli anni Ottanta*, Milano 2000
RIOUT, D., *L'arte del ventesimo secolo. Protagonisti, temi, correnti*, Torino 2000.
SCAGLIONE P., *Eur a Roma. Controguida d'architettura*, Roma 2000.
SALVATORI G., *Forme dell'utile e del superfluo: episodi di storia delle arti applicate in Campania dal 1920 al 1945*, in PICONE PETRUSA M. (a cura di), *Gli anni difficili. Arte a Napoli dal 1920 al 1945*, catalogo della mostra, (Napoli, Castelnuovo, 28 ottobre-5 dicembre 2000; Villa Pignatelli, 28 ottobre-3 dicembre 2000), Napoli 2000, pp. 77-83.
VALENTE I., *Grandi cicli decorativi a Napoli negli anni Trenta: un percorso fra la Stazione Marittima e la Mostra d'Oltremare*, in PICONE PETRUSA M. (a cura di), *Gli anni difficili. Arte a Napoli dal 1920 al 1945*, catalogo della mostra, (Napoli, Maschio Angioino, 28 ottobre-5 dicembre 2000; Villa Pignatelli, 28 ottobre-3 dicembre 2000), Napoli 2000, pp. 53-66.

2001
ALINOVI A., *Il Piano regolatore falsificato*, in ALINOVI A. (a cura di), *Il secolo breve di Mario Palermo*, Salerno 2001, pp. 335-344.
ARAMU L., *Dal Borgo di Fuorigrotta al Rione Flegreo*, Napoli 2001.
FRANZONE G., *"L'Africa generatrice e ispiratrice di poesia e arti" (F.T. Marinetti, 1938)*, in BARISIONE S., FOCHESSATI M., FRANZONE G. (a cura di), *Parole e immagini futuriste dalla Collezione Wolfson*, Milano 2001, pp. 50-64.
GENTILE, E., *Il culto del littorio*, Bari 2001.
LAMBERTUCCI, F., *Luigi Moretti. Cinema-teatro e piazza Imperiale all'E42, Roma*, Milano 2001.

2002
LABANCA, N., *Oltremare. Storia dell'espansione coloniale italiana*, Bologna 2002, pp. 220-261.
2003
BRAUN, E., *Mario Sironi. Arte e politica in Italia sotto il fascismo*, Torino 2003.
INSOLERA I., SETTE, A. M., *Roma tra le due Guerre. Cronache da una città che cambia*, Roma 2003.
MIGNEMI, A., *Lo sguardo e l'immagine. La fotografia come documento storico*, Torino 2003.
NAPOLITANO, G., *Giuseppe Macedonio e la ceramica d'architettura: l'Esedra della Mostra d'Oltremare*, in ROMITO, M. (a cura di), *La Ceramica di Posillipo (1937-1947). Un viaggio nell'immaginario e nella memoria della città di Napoli nella prima metà del Novecento*, «Quaderni della Ceramica», n. 1, Salerno 2003, pp. 104-109.
- *La Ceramica di Posillipo alla Triennale d'Oltremare nel 1940 a Napoli*, in ROMITO, M. (a cura di), *La Ceramica di Posillipo (1937-1947). Un viaggio nell'immaginario e nella memoria della città di Napoli nella prima metà del Novecento*, «Quaderni della Ceramica», n. 1, Salerno 2003, pp. 87-94.
- *La ceramica simbolista di Carlo Farneti*, in ROMITO, M. (a cura di), *La Ceramica di Posillipo (1937-1947). Un viaggio nell'immaginario e nella memoria della città di Napoli nella prima metà del Novecento*, «Quaderni della Ceramica», n. 1, Salerno 2003, pp. 23-24.
- *La maiolica d'artista: la Ceramica di Posillipo*, in ROMITO, M. (a cura di), *La Ceramica di Posillipo (1937-1947). Un viaggio nell'immaginario e nella memoria della città di Napoli nella prima metà del Novecento*, «Quaderni della Ceramica», n. 1, Salerno 2003, pp. 47-86.
ROMITO, M. (a cura di), *La Ceramica di Posillipo (1937-1947). Un viaggio nell'immaginario e nella memoria della città di Napoli nella prima metà del Novecento*, «Quaderni della Ceramica», n. 1, Salerno 2003.
SALVATORI G., *Nelle maglie della storia. Produzione artistico-industriale, illustrazione e fotografia a Napoli nel XX secolo*, Napoli 2003, pp. 51-82.
Schnapp J.T., *Anno X. La Mostra della rivoluzione fascista del 1932*, Ghezzano 2003.

2004

PETTENA, G., *Architettura e propaganda fascista nei filmati dell'Istituto Luce*, Roma 2004.

2005

BERTILACCIO, C., INNAMORATI, F., *Eur SpA e il patrimonio di E42*, Roma 2005

CARLI, C. F., MERCURIO, G., PRISCO, L. (a cura di), *E42 – EUR. Segno e sogno del Novecento*, catalogo della mostra, (Roma EUR, Palazzo degli Uffici, 1-30 aprile 2005), Roma 2005.

MARIANI, R., *Il luogo e il piano dell'E42*, in CARLI, C. F., MERCURIO, G., PRISCO, L. (a cura di), *E42 – EUR. Segno e sogno del Novecento*, catalogo della mostra, (Roma EUR, Palazzo degli Uffici, 1-30 aprile 2005), Roma 2005, pp. 26-27.

ROCHAT, G., *Le guerre italiane 1935-1943. Dall'impero d'Etiopia alla disfatta*, Torino 2005.

STENTI, S. (a cura di), *Marcello Canino 1895/1970*, catalogo della mostra, (Napoli, Palazzo Reale, 9 giugno-10 luglio 2005), Napoli 2005.

PICONE PETRUSA, M., *La pittura napoletana del '900*, Napoli 2005.

2007

ARENA G., *La Mostra d'Oltremare documento storico-artistico e monumento del XX secolo*, in AA. VV., *Per la conoscenza dei Beni Culturali: ricerche di dottorato*, S. Maria C.V. 2007, pp. 289-298.

GENTILE E., *Fascismo di pietra*, Roma-Bari 2007.

ROSPONI, C., (a cura di), *Eur Interrotta*, in «Aión», n. 16, 2007, pp. 120-135.

SALVATORI G., *Fra storia e cronaca: arte contemporanea e critica militante sulla stampa periodica degli anni '30*, in DI NATALE M.C. (a cura di), *Storia, critica e tutela dell'arte nel Novecento. Un'esperienza siciliana a confronto con il dibattito nazionale*, atti del convegno internazionale di studi in onore di Maria Accascina, Caltanissetta 2007, pp. 75-85.

VAJUSO, M., *E42 la gestione di un progetto complesso*, Roma 2007.

2009

Arena, G., *La Triennale d'Oltremare nella tradizione delle Esposizioni artistiche italiane del Novecento*, in AA.VV., *Per la conoscenza dei Beni Culturali II. Ricerche del dottorato in Metodologie conoscitive per la conservazione e la valorizzazione dei Beni Culturali 200-2009*, S. Maria C.V. 2009, pp. 243-256.

- *Unità delle Arti alla Prima Mostra Triennale delle Terre Italiane d'Oltremare*, in AA.VV., *L'art et la notion de civilisation*, Montréal 2009, p. 16.

BASILICO, A., *Il volto decorato dell'architettura. Napoli 1930-1940*, Napoli 2009.

DI LUGGO, A., CAMPI, M., *Palazzo Canino e la Mostra delle terre d'oltremare*, Roma 2009.

2011

ARENA, G., *Visioni d'Oltremare. Allestimenti e politica dell'immagine nelle esposizioni coloniali del XX secolo*, Napoli 2011.

- *Allestimenti e apparati decorativi alla Mostra d'Oltremare: Melkiorre Melis e il Padiglione Libia*, in «Napoli Nobilissima», vol. LXVIII, serie VI, vol. II, maggio-agosto 2011, pp. 137-152.

- *Gli allestimenti e le arti decorative della Mostra d'Oltremare*, in AA.VV., *La Ceramica del Novecento a Napoli, architettura e decorazione*, atti del convegno (Napoli, Palazzo Reale, 18 marzo 2011), Napoli 2011, pp. 223-261.

LUCIGNANO, D., CATULLO, S. (a cura di), *Giuseppe Macedonio scultore maiolicaro*, catalogo della mostra (Napoli, Castel dell'Ovo, 26 marzo-12 aprile 2011), Napoli 2011.

SALVATORI, G., *Il contributo delle arti applicate alla storia dell'arte contemporanea: il campione campano*, in AA.VV., *La Ceramica del Novecento a Napoli, architettura e decorazione*, atti del convegno (Napoli, Palazzo Reale, 18 marzo 2011), Napoli 2011, pp. 97-123.

2012

ARENA, G., *Napoli 1940-1952. Dalla Prima Mostra Triennale delle Terre Italiane d'Oltremare alla Prima Mostra Triennale del Lavoro Italiano nel Mondo*, Napoli 2012.

CIUCCI, G., LUX, S., PURINI, F., *Marcello Piacentini architetto 1881-1960*, Roma 2012.

2013

BENZI, F., *Arte in Italia tra le due guerre*, Torino 2013.

BERTELLA FARNETTI, P., MIGNEMI, A., TRIULZI, A., a cura di, *L'impero nel cassetto. L'Italia coloniale tra album privati e archivi pubblici*, Milano-Udine 2013.

2015

CUTRONI, F., *BBPR Palazzo delle poste, telegrafi e Te.ti all'E42*, Firenze 2015.

Printed by Books on Demand GmbH, Norderstedt / Germany